THE LORD'S PRAYER

MORE THAN A PRAYER

Dr. A. B. Brown, BA, M. Div., D. Min.

ISBN 978-1-0980-6959-9 (paperback)
ISBN 978-1-0980-6960-5 (digital)

Christian Faith Publishing, Inc.
832 Park Avenue
Meadville, PA 16335
www.christianfaithpublishing.com

Printed in the United States of America

To the Glory of God

This book is dedicated to my heavenly Father Who gave His beloved Son to take my place on Calvary and pay my infinite sin-debt I owed and could not pay. It is dedicated to my living loving Lord Who literally suffered my hell during those hours of darkness on the cross as He suffered and died as my substitute. Three days later, He rose from the dead and walked out of the grave victorious over death, hell, and the grave. Finally, it is dedicated to the Holy Spirit Who sought me out, convicted me, and drew me with bonds of love to Jesus. He regenerated me, indwelt me, and has been my Best Friend and Helper now for sixty-three years. This book is dedicated to the glory of God the Father, God the Son, and God the Holy Spirit, the great three in one, the one true and living God. He is the Lord God Almighty, Creator, Sustainer, and Controller of His creation and creatures. Of His own free choice, He chose me in Christ to be one of His elect children before He made the worlds. He alone is worthy of all the praise, honor, and glory of His creation and creatures.

To My Bride

This book is also dedicated to my precious bride of sixty-three years, Barbara, who has faithfully stood with me and encouraged me in the ministry. She has been my partner in the ministry, my best critic, and, above all things, my best and dearest friend. She has graciously sacrificed so much of our time together to the ministry of serving others and writing. Thank you so very much, Barb. I am deeply indebted to you, and next to Jesus, you are the love and the sunshine of my life.

—A. B. Brown

Introducing the Author

Dr. A. B. Brown was reared in a godly Christian home and saved at age nineteen. He has been married to his lovely wife, Barbara, for sixty-three years. They have two children, Greg and Susan, and five grandchildren.

Bro. Brown earned his BA from Welch College in Nashville, Tennessee. He graduated summa cum laude in 1969. He earned his M. Div. from Covenant Theological Seminary in St. Louis, Missouri, in 1973. At the age of seventy-two, he graduated from Liberty Baptist Theological Seminary with his D. Min. in 2010 with a 4.0 GPA.

Dr. Brown has pastored and taught theology on the college level for thirty years and served as the academic dean of a small Christian college for eleven years. He taught online courses on theology and the Bible at Liberty School of Divinity for ten years. Dr. Brown has remained actively involved in the ministry of the local church over the years serving as pastor, associate pastor, and interim pastor. He is presently serving as interim pastor and preaching three times almost every week at eighty-two years of age.

Ten reasons why you should read this book:

- One of the most *definitive explanations* of the *Lord's Prayer* in print

- Jesus's seven *perfect guides* on how to *pray* and *live*

- The most important *concept* in the human mind

- The most important *relationship* known to man

- The *authentic identity* of a child of God

- The most important *reason* for the Christian life

- The most important *role* of the Christian life

- The most important *rule* of the Christian life

- The most important *resource* of the Christian life

- How to live a *victorious* Christian life

Table of Contents

Introduction

The sixty-five words in the five verses of Mt. 6:9-13, which are universally known as The Lord's Prayer, have blessed countless millions down through the centuries. These words from the lips of our Lord have been set to music and have lifted the hearts of multiplied millions in praise and worship to God. This inspired passage has also been memorized and quoted as a prayer by the Father's children since it was labeled as The Lord's Prayer by Cyprian, bishop of Carthage around 350 AD.

There is certainly nothing wrong with quoting these verses as a prayer or singing them as a song of praise and worship to our awesome God. After all, they are a part of the inspired, inerrant, authoritative, powerful, transforming, and living Word of the living God. These sixty-five powerful words fell from the lips of our Lord, the Son of God. However, even after acknowledging these glorious truths, the fact remains that this passage is never quoted as a prayer or sung by anyone in the New Testament.

This fact does not mean that it is wrong to quote and sing this passage. It simply means that Jesus gave this passage as much more than a prayer. What is universally labeled as The Lord's Prayer was given by Jesus on two occasions and on both occasions it was given in a context of how to pray. In Mt. 6:9, Jesus introduces this prayer with the words,

"In this manner, therefore pray." In the Gospel of Luke, it was given in response to a request by one of Jesus's disciples. "Lord, teach us to pray as John also taught his disciples to pray." (Lk. 11:1).

The context of both these passages dictate that Jesus is giving instruction on *how* to pray and not on *what* to pray. Jesus took His disciples to the school of prayer by on the job training. They had heard Him pray on many occasions. They were aware that on special occasions He had prayed all night. Therefore, they were not asking for a short prayer of sixty-five words to be quoted as a ritual prayer. These men were seeking guidance on how to pray fervently and effectively like their Lord.

Jesus responds to this need by giving seven guiding principles on how to pray fervently and effectively. He was aware when He gave them that if believers prayed guided by them, they would soon live guided by them. Jesus understood the transformative power of prayer. Prayer does not change God. Prayer changes those who pray. How one prays determines how he lives, and this makes these prayer guides life guides.

It is obvious that if our Lord expects believers to know and pray to God as their Father, He also expects them to live like God is their Father. If He expects them to pray in subjection to their Father's will, He also expects them to live in subjection to His will. This same principle applies to each of Jesus's seven prayer guides. They are both prayer and life guides.

These seven guides are much more than a prayer because they also summarize seven core practices of the Christian life. First, a Christian is one who has come to know and pray to God as his Father. Second, a Christian prays and lives to glorify His Father's name as holy. Third, a Christian hallows his Father's name by praying and living to advance the coming of His kingdom rule in the hearts of men through evangelism. Fourth, a Christian prays and lives in subjection of his Father's will. Fifth, a Christian is totally dependent upon his heavenly Father for his daily bread and sustenance. Sixth, a Christian prays and lives forgiven by his heavenly Father while forgiving those who sin against him. Seventh, a Christian prays and lives guided by His heavenly Father and His deliverance from the temptations of sin and Satan.

In summary, these guides teach that a Christian is one who knows God as his Father, glorifies His name as holy, advances His Kingdom rule in the hearts of the lost through evangelism, lives in total reliance upon His Father, is a forgiven and forgiving person, and is guided and delivered by his heavenly Father. That is not an exhaustive description of what constitutes a Christian, but it does give the core traits and practices of a Christian.

These seven guides also give a balanced focus of the believer's prayers and life. They first focus *Upward* upon God then *Outward* upon others, and finally, they focus *Inward* upon self. This is the infinitely wise Son of God's divine focus of the Christian's prayers and his life. Any deviation from this balanced focus will have disastrous effects on everyone who tampers with this divine order.

By divine design, Jesus set a pattern of prayer before His disciples. He routinely took time from His busy schedule to rise before daybreak and go to His Secret Place to spend time alone with His Father in prayer (Mark 1:35). He spent all night in prayer before making the major decision to choose His twelve disciples (Luke 6:12–13). He prayed during the crisis hours before His arrest and crucifixion (Luke 22:39–46). As God, Jesus did not need to pray; but as a man, He needed to talk with His heavenly Father.

A vital part of the phenomenal success of the early church was primarily due to the priority they placed on prayer. The church was born out of a prayer meeting in the Upper Room (Acts 1:13–14, 2:1–4). It was in this prayer meeting that the anointing of the Holy Spirit came upon these praying people, and they spilled out on to the streets of Jerusalem with a passion for the perishing souls of men. They testified to the masses of the wonderful works of God which would include Calvary and the resurrection (Acts 2:3, 11).

Their anointed testimony in conjunction with the sound of the mighty rushing wind, which originated in a prayer meeting, resulted in the assembly of a large crowd of people. Then Peter, who had been anointed in this same prayer meeting, stood, raised his voice, and preached an anointed Bible-based message. Three thousand souls were saved, and the church prophesied by Jesus in Matthew 16:18 came into existence. As sovereign, God could have birthed His church apart from a prayer meeting, but He chose to birth His church out of a prayer meeting. We dare not miss this important point.

The apostles vocalized their priority on prayer when they asked to be relieved of ministering the widow's funds and said, "But we will give ourselves to prayer and to the ministry of the word" (Acts 6:4). These men had absorbed Jesus's priority on prayer and now viewed prayer and the ministry of the Word their primary pastoral responsibilities. The fact that they listed prayer first suggests that effective ministry of the Word must be preceded by prayer.

When Stephen was stoned to death, he died praying (Acts 7:59–60). When the church in Antioch needed to make an important decision about the church's first missionaries, they turned to God in prayer and fasting (Acts 13:1–3). Prayer is the antidote to worry and the path to peace (Phil. 4:6–7). Prayer is to characterize the Christian's life and worship (1 Thess. 5:17) to the point that the Lord's House should be known as a house of prayer (Isa. 56:7; Matt. 21:13; Mark 11:17; Luke 19:46). The modern church is known for many things, but few of them are known as houses of prayer.

Prayer is a priority with God because prayer is the highest act of worship of a believer. Prayer brings the believer to the end of himself and casts him in humility and faith upon every divine attribute of God. Prayer does not change the mind or heart of God. Prayer changes the mind and heart of the person who prays.

Prayer is more than a means of getting things from God; it is a means of getting God Himself. It is impossible to become a close personal friend of God without spending time alone with Him talking and fellowshipping with Him in the Secret Place. God does not place His hand of anointing on strangers. The intensity of one's prayers determines the intensity of God's anointing. There is no substitute for prayer.

The Lord's Prayer gives seven guides to keep believers from getting sidetracked in their prayers and in their Christian life. The devil and the flesh will distract believers into substituting the good for the best. The flesh is innately attracted to selfish things instead of glorifying the Father's name as holy by advancing His kingdom through evangelism. These guides help believers to keep the main thing the main thing.

It is important for believers to know that before Jesus gave His seven guides on the practice of powerful and effective prayer in Matthew 6:9–13, He gave four guides regulating the preparation of the heart for effective prayer in verses 5–8. These four laws express God's character that requires being before doing. How a person prays is determined by who he is in the deepest recesses of his being. In these four guides, God is saying that a person must be right before he can pray right.

5

First, he must be *sincere* when he prays. Sincere prayer rises from a heart free from all hypocrisy and deceit. A sincere heart does not seek to use prayer to con or use God for selfish and devious motives (verse 5). Second, powerful and effective prayer is *secret* prayer. It is in the Secret Place that believers are free to be completely open and honest with God. In the Secret Place, believers are completely free to express to their heavenly Father the deepest and secret longings and needs of their lives and their souls (verse 6).

Third, powerful and effective prayer is the *sure* prayer of faith. Sure prayer is the confident prayer of faith. This type of prayer rises from a heart that believes the Father will keep His promise and openly reward prayers addressed to Him in the Secret Place (verse 6). Fourth, powerful and effective prayer is *simple* prayer that avoids any attempt to impress God by eloquent lengthy prayers. God is far more concerned about the motives of the heart than how eloquently and lengthy these motives are expressed to Him.

These four guides on how to prepare the heart to pray powerfully and effectively can be summarized into the following critical truth about prayer. Powerful and effective prayer can only rise from an earnest heart that is completely open and honest with God and free from all deceit. This is the starting point of prayer that God honors.

We will now focus our attention on Jesus's first guide or law regarding knowing and relating to God as one's heavenly Father and how this great truth applies to our lives.

GOD AS FATHER

THE MOST IMPORTANT RELATIONSHIP KNOWN TO MAN

GUIDE NO. 1

Praying to and Living with God as My Father

Chapter 1

The Perception of God as Father

Our Father, which art in heaven
—Matthew 6:9 KJV

Our Father in heaven
—Matthew 6:9 NKJV

The Father of us, the [One] in the heavens
—Literal translation

Introduction

Bible Christianity is the only religion in the world that has a God Who personally relates to His followers in an intimate, caring Father-child relationship. Pagan deities do not establish intimate relationships with their subjects that reflect an authentic personal concern for their eternal welfare. This gracious loving Father-child relationship with born-again believers originated with the God of the Bible and is only found in Bible Christianity.

Jesus's mandate for believers to begin prayer by addressing God as their heavenly Father is not a legalistic mandate. Not every prayer in the

New Testament begins with the precise formula *Our Father in heaven*, but they do begin with some type of formal acknowledgment of the majesty and grandeur of God. This mandate to "Pause to praise before you pray" serves as a continuous restraint on the selfish heart of believers. Apart from this "Pause to praise," believers are inclined to rush into their Father's presence and launch into their list of requests without first pausing to remind themselves of the magnitude of the Person they are addressing.[1]

Jesus's focus in His first guide on God as the believers' loving heavenly Father does not diminish the importance of His holiness. This emphasis upon Him as a loving heavenly Father must be understood in its context as a guide on how to pray and live. Jesus was aware that believers would never become a people of prayer until they were convinced that, as their loving heavenly Father, He would hear and answer their prayers. The intimacy of this loving Father-child relationship met that critical need.

Jesus was aware of the necessity of keeping a balanced view of God as being first a holy God and then a loving God. Therefore, in His next guide, He will shift the focus to the holiness of God in His instruction

---

[1] When Peter and John were jailed by the Sanhedrin and released, they returned to their companions and called a prayer meeting and addressed their prayer to their "Lord." He obviously heard and responded since the place was shaken and they were filled afresh with the Holy Spirit and spoke the Word of God with boldness (Acts 4:23–31).

While dying as a martyr for his Lord, Stephen addressed his prayer to Jesus and requested, "Lord Jesus, receive my spirit" (Acts 7:59–60). After all, he was suffering martyrdom for his Jesus, and this would certainly incline him to call upon Jesus Who was no longer seated but was now standing watching the first martyr of the church die for His cause.

Paul addressed his prayer on the Damascus Road to Jesus when he cried out, "Who are You, Lord?" (Acts 9:5). However, he routinely addressed God in prayer as his Father (Eph. 1:17, 3:14, 5:20; Col. 1:3, 12, 3:17; 1 Thess. 1:3, 3:11).

for believers to pray and live to hallow their Father's name as holy. God created man in His image with the capacity for worship and fellowship. This intimate, loving Father-child relationship would serve as a key motivating factor for the Father's children to spend time fellowshipping with Him in prayer.

The concept of God as the believer's loving Father originated in the mind of God, not man. Knowing God as a loving Father by being born into His family by the new birth is the starting point of Bible Christianity. This is Practical Christianity 101. This Father-child relationship has several important spiritual implications, five of which are discussed below.

First, a person's concept of God is the most important thing about him.

Second, the plural possessive pronoun "our" limits those who are authorized to address God as Father in their prayers.

Third, the Father-child relationship of this guide is the expression of God's earnest desire for fellowship with man.

Fourth, this Father-child relationship is an expression of God's desire to meet man's deepest emotional need of love and acceptance.

Fifth, this Father-child relationship is an expression of God's desire to restore man's authentic identity as a child of God.

God as Father Is the Most Important Concept of the Believer's Mind

What comes to mind when a person thinks of the word "God" is the most important thing about him. People conform their lives to their concept of their God. If they perceive of God as a holy God, they tend to live a more holy life. On the other hand, if they perceive of God primarily as a gray-bearded old grandfatherly God Who loves everybody and punishes nothing, they will tend to live more carnal lives. An individual's perception of God determines how he perceives himself and how he lives.

An individual's worldview is determined by his view of God. If he views God as Creator, he will respect His authority over his life. On the other hand, if a person views himself as being a self-made person via the process of evolution, he will view God as being irrelevant to his life. This non-Creator God is an outsider Who has no right to intrude into his life. The self-made person is a law unto himself. He, and not God, makes the rules. He will, therefore, live guided only by his fallen, depraved reason. Once this transition of authority takes place, that person becomes his own god and bows to worship at the shrine of his deified self.

If it were possible to know with certainty a person's mental concept of God, it would be possible to predict his moral and spiritual life with great accuracy. Nothing shapes and molds a person's life and actions like his mental image of his God. What comes to mind when a person thinks the word "God" determines how he lives on planet earth and where he will spend eternity.

God as "Our" Father Limits Who Can Call God Their Father

The plural possessive personal pronoun "our" means that not everybody is authorized to address God as "their" Father. Only those born into His family by the new birth are authorized to address God as their Father. They are His spiritual children by spiritual birth. He chose them in Christ before creation (Eph. 1:4). After having chosen them in eternity past, in the process of time, He regenerated them by His Holy Spirit and gave them new life (Titus 3:5). It is only these "blood-bought" members of His family who are authorized to address God as "our" Father.

The Apostle John explains who is authorized to address God as Father when he writes, "He came to His own, and His own did not receive Him. *But as many as received Him, to them He gave the right to become children of God, even to those who believe in His name:* who were born, not of blood, nor of the will of the flesh, nor of the will of man, but of God" (John 1:11–13). Only those who "receive" Christ and "believe" in His name have the authority to address God as *our Father.* All others are excluded.

John returns to this subject in his first epistle where he is excited about the privilege of being one of the Father's children. He writes, "Behold, what manner of love the Father has bestowed on us, that we should be called children of God" (1 John 3:1)! John declares that the right and privilege of being called one of the children of God is an expression of His infinite love.

This plural form serves as a continual comfort and challenge to every believer. First, he is a member of the large and exclusive family, the family of God. Second, he is challenged to share the gospel to bring others into this large and exclusive family. It will be bliss indescribable to arrive home to spend eternity with the Father, the Son, and the Holy Spirit and fellowship with born-again members of His family. It will also be a thrill to spend eternity enjoying one's family inheritance on the new earth and in the majestic New Jerusalem.

An Expression of God's Earnest Desire
for Fellowship with Man

One of the most difficult truths of God's Word for believers to grasp is their heavenly Father's intense desire for fellowship with them. This is seen in the fact that God created man in His image as a social being with the capacity to socially interact in worship and fellowship with his Creator. Being God's only image-bearer makes man God's highest and most prized possession. Calvary is clear testimony to God's priority evaluation of man as His highest and most treasured creation. The fact that God made no provisions for the redemption of fallen angels is further evidence of His high esteem for man. Heaven, as a place of eternal fellowship between God and man, stands as God's striking testimony of His earnest desire for fellowship with man (Rev. 21:3–4).

The Greek word Jesus used for "father" is *pater*. The disciples would have understood this word to communicate the concept of a caring, loving Father. The word carried the idea of *the most respected person* in the home who had obligated himself to *provide* for and *protect* his children.

The parent-child relationship is the most intimate and loving relationship known to man. No other relationship could better express God's earnest desire for man's fellowship. The Father's intense desire for fellowship with His children has serious implications. Most importantly, it means that anywhere, anytime, and anyplace a believer pauses to enter the Secret Place and fellowship with His Father in prayer, He will gladly meet and fellowship with him.

This Intimate Father-Child Relationship Meets Man's Deepest Emotional Need

God created man in His image as a social being, and social beings have a deep need for love and acceptance. This is validated by Jesus's response to the question by a Pharisee asking the most important question known to man, "Above all things, what is God's number one desire or requirement of man?" (Matt. 22:36–40). Jesus replied, "Above all things, God requires you to love Him with all your heart, with all your soul, and with all your mind." As a social being, above all things, God desires to be loved.

Jesus immediately follows up God's number 1 requirement with His number 2 requirement. He declares, "And the second is like it, 'You shall also love your neighbor as yourself.'" Thus, as a social being, both God and man desire to be loved. Innate to the desire to be loved is the desire to be accepted. Therefore, the intense desire for love and acceptance is innate to social beings. The number 1 emotional need of everyone is to be loved and accepted.

This intense need means that being ostracized from the group creates all types of dangerous mental and emotional disorders. Every man, woman, boy, and girl needs to and seeks to "fit in." Every member of Adam's race desperately needs a sense of belonging that produces in them a sense of self-worth. The first responsibility of a parent to their child is to provide them love and acceptance. It is the responsibility of every believer to provide those around them with love and acceptance.

As the most loving and intimate relationship known to man, this Father-child relationship is designed by God to communicate the critical message of love and acceptance to everyone born into His family by the new birth. John 3:16 is the best known passage in the Bible because it cries out to a perishing world that God loves them so much that He gave His only Son to keep them from perishing. Calvary is God's declaration of His love and full acceptance of those who are born into His family by faith in His Son and His redemptive work.

One of the strongest fears of the human soul is the fear of not being loved and accepted by one's peers and by his God. Millions are enslaved by their fear of what others think about them. God has provided the only escape from this fear. He did this by His choice to relate to those born into His family in the most intimate relationship known to man, the parent-child relationship. This relationship between the redeemed and their heavenly Father provides them with the full love and acceptance they so desperately crave and need.

The devil works overtime to distort the believer's perception of being fully loved and accepted in Christ (Eph. 1:6). He uses the believer's awareness of his sinful nature and his failure to measure up to God's standard of perfect holiness (Matt. 5:48) to slowly and subtly distort his perception of God. The devil will use this awareness to convince the believer that God is a bit peeved with him. This gradual distortion of God from a smiling God to a frowning God will steal the believer's joy and victory. Apart from an understanding that they are fully loved and accepted in the Beloved, Satan will subtly convince the believer that he needs to work extra hard to earn his Father's favor.

The master of deception often steals a believer's joy and victory by creating in his mind a false image of God as an austere legalistic God Whose primary focus is on external morality. Worship of an angry austere legalistic God can never be a pleasurable relationship or worship experience. Beginning prayer by addressing God as one's loving heavenly Father is Jesus's way of constantly affirming believers as being fully loved and accepted by their heavenly Father.

It is a great day in the life of any believer when he realizes he cannot win what Jesus has already won for him. Jesus won the Father's eternal favor for His children by His sacrificial, substitutionary, satisfactory, atoning sacrifice of Himself on Calvary (Rom. 3:24; 2 Cor. 5:21; 1 Pet. 3:18; Isa. 53:4–6).[2]

His redemptive work paid for all the believer's sins, past, present, and future. When the Father's children are born into His family, He clothes them in the imputed righteousness of Christ which grants them God's permanent favor and approval (Phil. 3:9; Rom. 3:21–22). It is this full love and acceptance that also gives believers their sense of self-worth.

The Apostle Paul spoke eloquently to this divine favor earned by Jesus when he wrote,

> Blessed *be* the God and Father of our Lord Jesus Christ, who has blessed us with every spiritual blessing in the heavenly *places* in Christ, just as He chose us in Him before the foundation of the world, that we should be holy and without blame before Him in love, [5]having predestined us to adoption as sons by Jesus Christ to Himself, according to the good pleasure of His will, to the praise of the glory of His grace, *by which He [a]made us accepted in the Beloved.* (Eph. 1:3–6)

---

[2] The Greek word used by Jesus on the cross when He shouted "It is finished" (*tetelestai*) could simply refer to bringing something to its conclusion. It could also be used as a commercial term having reference to a debt being paid in full. As used by Jesus, His death and resurrection marked the conclusion of His redemptive work. However, it also meant that the sin-debt man owed and could not pay had been paid in full by His atoning sacrifice.

Oh yes, the heavenly Father can be angered by the sins of His children, but His wrath does not wipe the smile from His face. A loving Father can punish His wayward children with a smile because His discipline is an expression of His infinite and enduring love for His children (Heb. 12:3–11). The Father's perfect anger is always designed for His glory and the good of His children.

This positive perception of being fully loved and accepted by God as a loving, smiling heavenly Father changes everything. It makes worship a pleasurable experience. The smile of His unchanging love and acceptance changes serving Him from a duty to a joy. God's smile adds sunshine to one's life that nothing else can replicate. His smile is an added attraction of heaven. God's smile of love and acceptance puts a smile on the face of His children giving them a sense of purpose and self-worth that is contagious to a perishing world.

This Father-Child Relationship Restores the Believer's Authentic Identity

This first guide provides the believer with the most important concept in his mind which is his perception of God as his heavenly Father. This guide also provides him with what may be the second most important concept in his mind which is his perception of himself. Every believer needs the positive perception of himself as being one of the Father's fully loved and accepted children. This positive self-image involves the complete restoration of his identity which was marred by the fall. Because of Christ's redemptive work on Calvary, believers can join with John as he shouts, "Behold, now are we the children of God!" (1 John 3:2).

Until a person is born into the Father's family by the regenerative work of the Holy Spirit (Titus 3:5), he is spiritually dead in trespasses and sin (Eph. 2:1, 5). His mind is blinded by the god of this world making him unable to discern his real identity (2 Cor. 4:3–4). He thinks he is alive, but he is dead (Eph. 2:1, 5). He thinks he can see, but he is blind (2 Cor. 4:3–4). He thinks he is free, but he is a slave to sin and Satan (John 8:32–36). He thinks he is good, but he is bad (Rom. 3:10–12). Only those born into the family of God by the new birth have their authentic identity completely restored.

The statement "I will never know who I am, until I meet the Great I Am" is a valid biblical truth. When one is born into the family of God, he regains his original identity as an authentic child of God who is fully loved and accepted. For the first time in his life, he can see himself for who he is. He is a *unique* and *special* creation of God that sets him apart from all others. There has never been, nor will there ever be, another person like him. He is a unique work of God's grace with a unique role in life that nobody can duplicate.

He may have gifts and talents like other believers, but when mixed with his unique personality, they also become unique. As one of the Father's children, he has a role to fill in His kingdom work that nobody in all of creation can perform like him. Others may do the same thing, but they cannot do it as he can due to his unique personality. The believer's unique personality and role give him a unique identity, purpose, and self-worth.

Without pride, the Father's children can boast and say, "By my Father's saving and transforming grace, He has made me into somebody who is unique and special. I am fully loved and accepted by my heavenly Father. He chose me in Christ as one of His children before He created the world. My name is recorded in the Lamb's Book of Life. Jesus knew my name when He hung on Calvary. I am somebody who is very important to God." These are strutting rights of the Father's children based on His amazing grace and not on human pride.

It is a great day in the life of a believer when he realizes who he is in Christ. It is a great day when he is freed from worry over what his peers think about him and realizes that he is fully loved and accepted by the most important and influential Person ever to exist. His self-worth is determined by his heavenly Father and not by his peers and by this world.

When a person trusts Christ and becomes one of the Father's children, the restoration of his identity as a child of God is incomplete. The restoration of the rest of his forfeited identity and inheritance will be completed when he lands on the new earth and walks through the gates of pearl onto the streets of gold. Then he will have his purified and glorified resurrection body fashioned after his Lord's resurrected body (Phil. 3:21). He will once again live in a sin-free environment and enjoy perfect harmony and fellowship with his Lord that was forfeited at the fall (Rev. 21:3–4, 22:3).

Modern evolutionary humanists suffer from a major identity crisis. They live in an evolving godless mechanized world created and controlled by natural law. Their naturalistic world is a closed system that excludes any intervention of the supernatural. Humanists live in a world owned and operated by natural law that came into existence without a law-giver. This mystical self-originating law could cease to function at any moment, and they and their world would implode. Their evolving world robs them of the possibility of absolute truth, morality, and hope.

Evolution reduces men to living breathing chemical blobs that are an accident of nature. At best, men are soulless purposeless animals living on a giant mechanical device that is the result of a mindless explosion. The complex and organized body they live in and the complex and organized world they inhabit are both self-created and self-maintaining apart from an intelligent designer and sustainer. Their godless mechanized world of chance offers no basis for purpose and hope as man marches briefly across the stage of time back into the nothingness from whence he came.

In striking contrast to the gloom and doom of humanism, the members of the Father's family have purpose and hope in this life and for eternity to come. Because they are His children, they know *who they are*. Because they are made in the image of God, they know *how they got here*. Because the Father's children are called to live to the glory of God, they know *why they are here*. Finally, because their names are written in the Lamb's Book of Life, the Father's children know *where they are going when they die*. Their lives have meaning, purpose, and hope.

Jesus identified all people as being members of one of two families with two very different fathers. When He instructed His followers to address God as *Our Father in heaven*, He defined all those born into the Father's family by the new birth as His children. The Apostle John refers to this unique privilege granted only to those who "receive and believe" as "born of God." He wrote

> He was in the world, and He made the world, and the world did not know Him. He came to His own, and His own did not receive Him. But as many as *received Him*, to them He gave the *right* to become children of God, even to those who *believe* in His name: who were *born*, not of blood, nor of the will of the flesh, nor of the will of man, but *of God*. (John 1:10–13)

Jesus defined humanity's second family as the devil's family. He then gave some details about the abhorrent character of the father of this family in the following passage:

> …If God were your Father, you would love Me, for I proceeded forth and came from God; nor have I come of Myself, but He sent Me. Why do you not understand My speech? Because you are not able to listen to My word. *You are of your father the devil, and the desires of your father you want to do.* He was a murderer from the beginning and does not stand in the truth, because there is no truth in him. When he speaks a lie, he speaks from his own *resources*, for he is a liar and the father of it. (John 8:42–44)

The abhorrent character and destiny of the devil and his family makes being identified as a member of the family of God the most important mark of identity known to man. It restores to the believer his authentic identity as a child of God and the blessings forfeited by Adam at the fall.

Conclusion

The perception of God as Father is the most important thing about any child of God. This relationship determines their worldview and their eternal destiny. Knowing God as Father provides His children with the correct perception of who they are and their sense of self-worth. This Father-child relationship is the most important, intimate, and enduring relationship known to man.

It is the starting point of everything spiritual and is foundational to Practical Christianity 101.

Life Lessons
"OUR FATHER IN HEAVEN"

Only those born into God's family by the new birth are the authorized to pray to Him as their Father.

Only the Father's children know who they are, how they got here, why they are here, and where they are going when they die.

Only the Father's children know that they are fully and unconditionally loved and accepted in Christ.

The Holiness of God Is His Perfect Purity

GUIDE NO. 2

Praying and Living to Glorify My Father's Name as Holy

THE MAJESTY OF HIS GLORY
AND THE GLORY OF HIS MAJESTY

It is impossible for unholy people to glorify a holy God.
Oh, worship the Lord in the beauty of holiness.
As He Who has called you is holy, you
also be holy in all your conduct.

Chapter 2

The Priority of the Father's Holiness

Hallowed be Your name
—Matthew 6:9

Let Your name be sanctified, honored,
or reverenced as holy.
—Literal translation

Introduction

Jesus's first guide focuses upon the believer's *loving* Father. His second guide shifts His focus to the believer's *holy* Father. In doing this, Jesus moves to guarantee a biblically balanced view of God as both a holy and a loving Father. This balance is necessary due to the natural tendency of the depraved heart to emphasize the love of God above His holiness. The depraved heart is naturally inclined toward sin. Unless it is checked by divine restraints like this second guide, it will continually seek to create for itself a loving permissive God Who will tolerate its sin.

These two guides serve as counterbalances to each other. Love unguided by holiness will always degenerate into permissiveness, while holiness unguided by love will always degenerate into cold dead legalistic orthodoxy. God's holiness and love can never be separated. Neither can God's love ever be exalted above His holiness, which is God's number 1 moral trait or attribute. That priority can never be reversed without serious consequences.

This second guide instructs the Father's children to think, pray, and live in a manner to reverence their Father's name as holy. The practice of reverencing His name as holy must become the guide of the believer's thoughts, prayers, and life. They are to think holy thoughts, pray holy prayers, and live holy lives. Having been born into their Father's family by the new birth, His children should resemble their Father in holiness. Holiness should characterize their lives as it characterizes their Father's life. It is impossible for unholy people to reverence God's name as holy.

The word translated as "hallowed" communicates the idea *Let Your name be hallowed, sanctified, reverenced, and awed as holy*. The root word underlying this Greek verb has as its core meaning "holy." The Holy Spirit inspired Matthew to choose this exact verb form because He wanted to emphasize the point of hallowing the Father's name as holy. This fact becomes very important in an age where much of the church with its false-positive gospel of love has almost banned the words *holy, sin*, and *hell* from the American pulpit.

Anything that glorifies God as holy is good for man. Because He is above all things a holy God, He has made holiness the moral condition necessary for man's highest good. The holier a person is, the happier he will be. It is a fixed and unalterable law of God that "holiness brings happiness and sin brings sorrow." Holiness exalts a culture, and sin debases it. Holiness brings law and order, and sin brings crime and chaos. Holiness is the moral condition necessary for the blessings of God resulting in the well-being of man and his culture.

When the original language of Jesus's second guide is considered in its historical, cultural, and grammatical settings, this guide, *Hallowed be Your name*, has the following applications to the Christian life.

The meaning of the word "hallowed" in the original prioritizes the holiness of God.

The mandate *Hallowed be Your name* demands a deep sense of awe or reverence.

The concept *Hallowed be Your name* demands a God-centered life.

The priority Jesus places on *hallowing the Father's name as holy* makes His remaining guides, His instructions on how to best glorify the Father's name, as holy.

The Priority of Holiness

The Greek verb translated as "hallowed" is derived from a noun which has "holiness" as its core meaning. [3] The form of this Greek verb would

---

[3] The word *hagios* occurs 230 times in the New Testament and is translated as "holy" 176 times. In ninety of these instances, it is translated as a part of the name of the "Holy" Spirit. *Hagios* is also translated as "saints" fifty-four times. When translated as "saints," the emphasis is upon them being separated from sin and this world unto God Who is above all things a holy God. Because the noun *hagios* bears the core meaning of holy, the word when translated as "saint" suggests not being contaminated by sin. Ultimately, it designates a person as being character-ized as a holy person.

The verb form of the noun *hagios* is the word *hagiazo*. This is the word translated as "hallowed." It is used twenty-eight times in the New Testament. It is translated as "sanctified" in twenty-six of its twenty-eight uses. The two times it is not trans-

be translated literally as *Let Your name be sanctified, honored, or reverenced as holy.* God is indeed a loving God, but because holiness is His primary moral attribute, He has chosen that He first be hallowed as holy and then as loving. This is consistent with the testimony of the Scriptures which exalts His holiness as His number 1 moral attribute.

Although the Word of God prioritizes God's holiness above His love, holiness has fallen on hard times in recent decades. The rage of the age is a positive, feel-good, false gospel that minimizes God's holiness and exalts His love. The new American God is a permissive God of love Who is soft on sin. This shift reflects a serious lack of understanding that God's love is an overflow of His holiness.

In a day of biblical ignorance, the holiness of God is best defined as the *Perfect Purity* of God who is free from any contamination or imperfection in His essence, being, motives, thoughts, words, and deeds. This perfect purity frees God from any contamination of any kind in His essence, being, thoughts, motives, words, and deeds. His perfect purity will always express itself in the perfect good which is always the highest good. This highest good expressed toward man is called the love of God.

Therefore, God's love is the outworking and overflow of His perfectly pure thoughts, motives, words, and deeds which expresses themselves toward man in always seeking his highest good. Theologically, it is impossible to reverse the order and exalt God's love over His holiness.

---

lated as "sanctifies" are here in Matthew 6:9 and its parallel passage in Luke 11:2 where it is translated as "hallowed." When translated as "sanctified," the idea is to set someone or something apart from the mundane as holy. It is translated in Revelation 22:11 as "let Him be holy." The passive form of the verb as used in Matthew 6:9 literally means "Let Him be set apart or reverenced and regarded as holy."

It can be done in practice, but it constitutes a reversal of God's nature and will always have tragic consequences.

Holiness that diminishes God's love leads to legalism or a cold dead orthodoxy. Love that diminishes God's holiness leads to carnality. By their holy or godly lives, Christians win the respect of the world. By their loving compassion, they win the heart of the world. The two are inseparable and irreversible.

God's priority on His holy nature is seen in the fact that before creation, He chose His children to live *holy* and *blameless* lives to the *praise of His glory and grace*. Paul wrote:

> Blessed *be* the God and Father of our Lord Jesus Christ, who has blessed us with every spiritual blessing in the heavenly *places* in Christ, just as He chose us in Him before the foundation of the world, that we should be holy and without blame before Him in love, having predestined us to adoption as sons by Jesus Christ to Himself, according to the good pleasure of His will, to the praise of the glory of His grace, by which He made us accepted in the Beloved. (Eph. 1:3–6)

The God Isaiah saw in his vision in Isaiah chapter 6 was a holy God. He saw the Seraphim, who were angelic beings, as they sang "Holy, holy, holy is the Lord of hosts; the whole earth is full of His glory." In the Hebrew language, the triple repetition of the word "holy" was the most emphatic way they had of placing a strong emphasis upon God being first and foremost a holy God.

This triple emphasis is repeated in the New Testament when John saw the Cherubim surrounding the throne. They are probably the highest order of angels. John was impressed by their song of praise to God as they sang, "Holy, holy, holy, Lord God Almighty, Who was and is and is to come!" (Rev. 4:8).

The Psalmist connects glorifying God with worshiping Him in the beauty of His holiness. He writes, "Give unto the Lord the glory due His name, worship the Lord in the beauty of holiness" (Ps. 29:2, 96:9). God occupies "the throne of His holiness" (Ps. 47:8). God emphasizes His holiness in His declaration, "For thus says the Lofty One, who inhabits eternity, whose name is holy, I dwell in the holy place" (Isa. 57:15). This guide to hallow the Father's name as holy is in keeping with the fact that, above all things, God is a holy God.

Any representation of God that exalts His love above His holiness is idolatry. It is to create in one's mind an imaginary god who only exists in the mind that created him. This imaginary god has no objective reality. He is not the God they will face on the Judgment Day.

It is still true that God is holy, sin is bad, hell is hot, and sinners desperately need to be saved.

A Deep Sense of Awe

Jesus mandated this holy awe of God by His use of the Greek word *hagiazo*, which is translated as "hallowed." As a passive verb, *hagiazo* could literally be translated "Let Your name be reverenced as holy." The disciples would have readily understood Jesus to be instructing them to approach God in prayer and in life with a deep sense of awe.

This deep sense of awe or reverence also grew out of the Jewish culture. As Jews, the disciples would have already had a deep sense of awe for the name of God. Over the centuries, the Jews had developed a reverence for the name of God that bordered on the extreme. God had revealed Himself to Moses and the Jews in Exodus 3:14 by the name of YHWH which is a Hebrew state of being (verb), denoting continuous action suggesting the eternality of God.[4] Most English translations render it as "I am that I am" which communicates the idea of continuity.

Devout Jews ceased to pronounce the name YHWH in oral speech. This tradition stemmed from the command of God in the book of Exodus that forbids taking His name in vain. The command states, "You shall not take the name of the LORD your God in vain, for the LORD will not hold him guiltless who takes His name in vain" (Exod. 20:7). God is clear that taking His name in vain is a personal offense for which He will hold the guilty party accountable.

To avoid the guilt and curse of using God's name in vain, they refused to pronounce the name YHWH. When the Jews came across God's name in Scripture, they substituted the word *Adonai* which is the general word for Lord. English translations continued this trend by translating YHWH as LORD (with all caps). The most notable exception is the *American Standard Version*, which transliterated the divine name as Jehovah. Many English-speaking Jews today write "G-d" instead of spelling out the whole word God.

This existing reverence for the name of God is evident in the Gospel of Matthew. As a Jew, who was addressing his gospel to Jews, Matthew often avoided the use of the name God in the phrase *kingdom of*

---

[4]   In Hebrew, the name of God consists of the four letters YHWH sometimes called the *tetragrammaton* (Greek word for "four letters").

God and substituted "God" with the term "heaven." There are parallel instances when Luke and Mark used the term *kingdom of God* to refer to the same kingdom that Matthew referred to as the kingdom of heaven. He did this out of deference to the Jewish tradition of avoiding the use of the name of God.

This deep sense of awe would include a healthy fear of God. This is not a fear that brings terror. It is a healthy fear growing out of a deep respect of God as a holy and loving Father Who will chastise His erring children for His glory and their good. Proverbs recognizes the fear of God as *the beginning of wisdom* (Prov. 9:10).

This healthy fear is illustrated in the book of Acts in the incident involving Ananias and Sapphira's attempt to deceive the Holy Spirit in holding back a part of their offering. This incident took place during the founding days of the church. It was necessary for God to create among Christians a healthy awe and respect for His church as His newly founded divine institution. (He had done the same thing in the Old Testament in the incident of killing Nadab and Abihu in Leviticus 10:1–3. The strange fires they offered reflected a serious lack of respect for the Tabernacle which also had recently been founded.)

In both instances, God killed two people for their lack of respect for His newly founded divine institutions. Luke explains the result of God killing Ananias and Sapphira when he writes, "And great fear came on all the church and on all who heard these things" (Acts 5:11). In his explanation of God killing Nadab and Abihu, Moses told Aaron their father, "This is what the LORD spoke, saying 'By those who come near Me I must be regarded as holy; And before all the people I must be glorified.' So, Aaron held his peace" (Lev. 10:3).

The author of Hebrews explains the basis of a healthy fear of God based upon both His holiness and His love when he writes:

> And you have forgotten the exhortation which speaks to you as to sons: "My son, do not despise the chastening of the LORD, NOR BE DISCOURAGED WHEN YOU ARE REBUKED BY HIM; FOR WHOM THE LORD LOVES HE CHASTENS, and scourges every son whom He receives." If you endure chastening, God deals with you as with sons; for what son is there whom a father does not chasten? But if you are without chastening, of which all have become partakers, then you are illegitimate and not sons. Furthermore, we have had human fathers who corrected *us,* and we paid *them* respect. Shall we not much more readily be in subjection to the Father of spirits and live? For they indeed for a few days chastened *us* as seemed *best* to them, but He for *our* profit, that *we* may be partakers of His holiness. Now no chastening seems to be joyful for the present, but painful; nevertheless, afterward it yields the peaceable fruit of righteousness to those who have been trained by it. (Heb. 12:5–11)

God's holiness dictates that sin be punished. His love dictates that it be administered with tender compassion for the ultimate good of His children. He chastises them to help them avoid the catastrophic consequences of sin. His chastisement is also a sign that they are His genuine children and not illegitimate children.

One of the explanations of the carnal Christianity of modern America is her loss of any healthy awe and fear of a holy God Who will chastise them because He loves them. American Christians need to once again perceive of God as a holy God and then as a loving God. It will be only as the church returns to the holy God revealed in the Bible that she will develop a healthy fear of God that produces a fear of and a departure from sin. Proverbs declares that "by the fear of the LORD ONE DEPARTS FROM EVIL" (Prov. 16:6).

A God-Centered Life

In the four words *Hallowed be Your name*, Jesus makes the Christian life a God-centered life and the Christian religion a God-centered religion. It is impossible to pray and live to hallow God's name as holy in thoughts, motives, words, and deeds apart from living a God-centered life. In the four words *Hallowed be Your name*, Jesus issues a warning that God cannot be conned.

God refuses to be used only as fire insurance, a personal rescue squad, or a Mr. Fix It, although He is indeed all of these. Before any of these, Jesus is demanding a God-centered life that first focuses on hallowing His name as holy.

Below is a forceful paraphrase of what Jesus is saying to the Father's children:

> Up to this point, you have lived your lives to honor and glorify your name; but now that you have been to Calvary and come to know God as your heavenly Father, those days are over. It is no longer all about you; it is now all about your heavenly Father and the honor and glory of His name. As one of the Father's children, you are now to think, pray, and live in a manner to hallow and glorify His name

as holy before a perishing world. Every thought, motive, word, or deed is measured by the question, "Will it glorify my heavenly Father's name as holy?" Instead of your former me-centered life, *your life is now to be a God-centered life!*

One test of the authenticity of one's profession of faith is where the glory of God fits into his life. This question could also be formulated as follows: "Is my life all about glorifying my name, or is it all about glorifying His name?" In a truly God-centered life, the honor and glory of His name as holy becomes the driving force of life. Every thought, motive, word, or deed is measured by whether it will hallow the Father's name as holy. This can never happen apart from being born into the family of God by the new birth and being indwelled by the Holy Spirit. The spirit then floods his heart with a supernatural ability to love God and put Him first (Rom. 5:5).

Jesus's Guides on How to Best Hallow His Father's Name

Glorifying the Father's name as holy does not get much traction in today's carnal Church. However, it is important enough to Jesus to rank as number 2 on His list of seven guides on how Christians are to think, pray, and live. In His second guide, Jesus summarizes Practical Christianity 101 into the four words *Hallowed be Your name*. Jesus ultimately summarizes the Christian life into "the glory of God." In Jesus's logic, a person must first come to know God as his Father. Once this happens, the driving force of his life then becomes to glorify his Father's name as holy.

After complying with Jesus's first guide, His second guide—to hallow one's Father's name as holy—then moves to the top of His list and becomes Jesus' number 1 priority for how believers are to pray and live. Glorifying the Father's name as holy then becomes the driving force of his thoughts, prayers, and life. According to 2 Corinthians 5:17, believers are to *do all things* to glorify God.

In His remaining guides, Jesus proceeds to give instructions on the five ways to best glorify the Father's name as holy. Coming from the mind of infinite wisdom, these are the five best ways, but obviously not the only ways.

The order of these remaining guides only makes sense as one understands that Jesus is addressing believers and not the unsaved. Otherwise, He would have placed doing the will of God before advancing the coming of His kingdom rule and authority through evangelism. The logic is to first evangelize and then those born into His family will be subject to His will. That order cannot be reversed. The unsaved have no interest in doing God's will.

The unsaved are unholy, and unholy people cannot glorify the name of a holy God as holy. Therefore, Jesus places advancing the coming of the Father's kingdom rule and authority in the hearts of the unsaved before He instructs them that the Father's children best glorify their Father's name as holy by doing His will.

Holiness is conformity to the will of God revealed in the Word of God. As previously cited, Peter clearly ties holiness to obeying the will of God when he writes, "As obedient children, not conforming yourselves to the former lusts, as in your ignorance, but as he who has called you is holy, you also be holy in all your conduct. Because it is written, 'Be holy, for I am holy'" (1 Pet. 1:14–16). The author of Hebrews writes, "Pursue peace with all men, and holiness, without which no one will see the Lord" (Heb. 12:14).

Only those born into the Father's family by the new birth become His children who are authorized to address Him in prayer as their Father. Only those who know God as their Father can pray and live to glorify their Father's name as holy. One of the very best ways to hallow the Father's name as holy is by advancing the coming of His kingdom rule and authority through evangelism.

They glorify His name as holy through evangelism because they think, pray, and live subject to their Father's will while being totally dependent upon Him for everything.

Since unholy people cannot glorify a holy God's name as holy, believers need daily cleansing through their Father's forgiveness. They also need to model Christ and glorify His name before a perishing world by readily forgiving those who sin against them.

Finally, only those whose lives are characterized by overcoming temptation can hallow their Father's name as holy. It is impossible for the unforgiven who refuse to forgive to hallow the Father's name as holy through evangelism.

The Father's name is best hallowed as holy by putting these guides into shoe leather and living them out in one's daily life before a perishing world.

The world does need to hear the gospel, but they need to see the gospel exemplified by those who live holy lives guided by Jesus's subsequent guides on how best to hallow the Father's name as holy.

Life Lessons
"HALLOWED BE YOUR NAME"

Holiness is God's number 1 moral attribute.

Holiness is God's perfect purity in His essence, thoughts, motives, words, and deeds.

Glorifying the Father's name as holy summarizes the Christian life.

Unholy people cannot glorify a holy God.

Holiness brings happiness and sin brings sorrow.

God blesses the righteous and curses the wicked.

The Kingdom Is the Kingdom Rule
and Authority of King Jesus

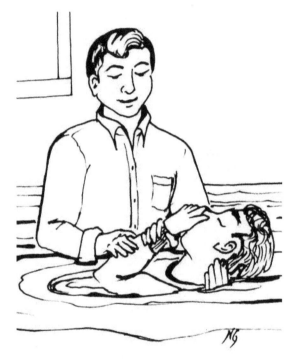

"Advancing the Coming of the
Kingdom through Evangelism"

GUIDE NO. 3

Praying and Living to Advance the Coming of the Kingdom

Chapter 3

A Passion for Advancing
the Father's Kingdom

Your kingdom come
—Matthew 6:10

Let Your kingdom come.
—Literal translation

Let Your kingdom rule and authority
come into the hearts of men.
—Literal interpretation

Introduction

The three words *Your kingdom come* suggest that there is a real kingdom with a real King, but it has not fully arrived. It is still a coming kingdom. It is a dynamic kingdom that is here, but it is not fully here. The full and final manifestation of this glorious kingdom is fixed and certain, but its final two stages or phases come on God's sovereign timing.

This coming kingdom was the focal point of Jesus's preaching. Mark wrote, "Now after John was put in prison, Jesus came to Galilee, preaching the gospel of the Kingdom, and saying, 'The time is fulfilled, and the kingdom of God is at hand. Repent, and believe in the gospel'" (Mark 1:14–15). Matthew wrote, "From that time Jesus began to preach and to say, 'Repent, for the Kingdom of Heaven is at hand'… And Jesus went about all Galilee, teaching in their synagogues, preaching the gospel of the kingdom, and healing all kinds of sickness and healing all kinds of disease among the people" (Matt. 4:17, 23).

In these passages, Jesus makes five bold assertions about this kingdom.

First, the kingdom was a priority in the preaching of Jesus.

Second, He came to make kingdom Christians who are united in advancing the coming of the rule and authority of their King in the hearts of men.

Third, entrance to the kingdom required *repentance* and *belief* in the gospel. Jesus declared that those who believe are born again and can enter the kingdom (John 3:3, 5).[5]

Fourth, Jesus's declaration that the kingdom was *at hand* meant that it was available and accessible.

---

[5] Genuine faith always involves repentance. They are opposite sides of the same coin. Jesus would not tell people in Mark 1:14–15 that they had to repent and believe the gospel to get into the kingdom and then change the rules in those passages where only belief is mentioned. Jesus never contradicts Himself, and He teaches that those who do not repent perish (Luke 13:5) and those who do not believe also perish (John 3:16). Therefore, those passages which only mention one of these requirements assume the other.

Fifth, as a dynamic kingdom that was already present but still coming, the kingdom comes in three phases or stages.

If the three words *Your kingdom come* are interpreted by their literary and historical contexts, they communicate the following three great spiritual truths about the kingdom:

First, the personal possessive pronoun *Your* makes God the exclusive and sovereign owner of the kingdom.

Second, the primary meaning of the Greek word translated as *kingdom* is "the rule and authority of the king" which *comes* in the hearts and lives of men through evangelism.

Third, the word *come* makes the Father's kingdom a dynamic kingdom that is present but still coming.

The Proprietor of the Kingdom

Jesus did not instruct believers to pray *"the" kingdom come*. He instructed them to pray *"Your" kingdom come*. Jesus used the possessive pronoun "Your" to emphasize God's ownership of the kingdom. He is the sole proprietor. There are no stockholders and no board of directors. It is not a democracy controlled by the vote of the majority. As the Creator of the kingdom and the Redeemer of its citizens, God is the sole owner and operator of His kingdom.

There will be no illegal immigrants or aliens in His kingdom. Nobody will ever walk undetected through the gates of pearl. They can never slip past the "all-seeing" eye of an omniscient (Ps. 147:5) and omnipresent King (Jer. 23:24). He knows every citizen of His kingdom by name and is personally acquainted with each of them. He purchased their redemption on Calvary. Every citizen is His by rights of both creation and redemption. As sovereign King of kings and Lord of lords, God owns and operates His kingdom by His sovereign good pleasure.

The Priority of the Kingdom

Denominations can serve a useful function in the body of Christ. However, most churches are far more focused on denominational Christianity than kingdom Christianity. The tragic result is the fragmentation of the body of Christ that severely limits the church's ability to join hands in reaching a lost world with the gospel.

Jesus did not come preaching that the Baptist, Methodist, or Presbyterian denominations were at hand. He came preaching that the kingdom of God was at hand. When a person is born again, he is not born into a denomination; he is born into the kingdom of God. The church is charged with the responsibility of advancing the coming of the kingdom, not the perpetuation of a denomination.

The kingdom of God takes precedence over denominationalism and institutionalism. Advancing this kingdom through evangelism takes priority over the petty differences that so tragically fragment the body of Christ. Denominations are not innately sinful until denominational loyalty takes precedence over kingdom loyalty. When denominational distinctives, which do not affect the fundamental doctrines of the faith, keep believers from uniting to evangelize the world, then denominational loyalty has become a sin and a hindrance to advancing the kingdom of God.

The Perpetuation of the Kingdom

In establishing what Jesus means by the three words *Your kingdom come*, three things are necessary. First, it will be necessary to establish what Jesus meant when He used the word *kingdom.* How does biblical use define the kingdom? Second, it will be necessary to define what He meant by the word *come.* How does the kingdom come? Third, it will be necessary to analyze how Jesus went about advancing the coming of His kingdom while incarnate.

First, the word translated as "kingdom" is *basileia.* This Greek word is used 162 times in the New Testament. The primary meaning of this word has to do with the *royal rule* and *authority* of a king over his kingdom. The secondary meaning of this word has to do with the *subjects* and *the domain* over which the king rules. This suggests that Jesus used the word concerning the rule and authority of the King in the hearts and lives of His subjects.

The Old Testament book of Daniel speaks of this kingdom rule and authority in the following passage:

> And there was given him (King Jesus) dominion (rule and authority), and glory, and a kingdom, that all people, nations, and languages, should serve him: his dominion is an everlasting dominion, which shall not pass away, and his kingdom which shall not be destroyed... But the saints of the Most High shall receive the kingdom, and possess the kingdom forever, even forever and ever. (Dan. 7:14, 18)

Daniel emphasizes the rule and authority of the King by making His dominion a key element of the kingdom. This dominion is explained by the fact that *all people, nations, and languages should serve Him.* He further affirms the importance of this kingdom rule and authority when he emphasizes that it is everlasting. Daniel wrote, "His dominion is an everlasting dominion, which shall not pass away."

Second, the Greek word that is translated as "come" is derived from the root word *erkomai* which has the primary meaning of to *come* or *go.* The form of this verb in the original is a command, but because finite men cannot command an infinite God, it is interpreted as an urgent plea to *let Your kingdom come.*

When these two words are combined and interpreted according to their primary meanings, they constitute an urgent plea to let His kingdom rule and authority in the hearts of men come. This plea would include the idea that when the rule and authority of the King comes into the hearts of men, the kingdom itself comes.

Third, as the ideal Christian, Jesus's method of advancing the coming of His kingdom must serve as the divine guide on how believers are to advance the coming of the kingdom. When Jesus repeatedly spoke of the kingdom being "at hand" (Matt. 4:17, 23), He was urging those who heard Him to *repent* and *believe* in the gospel in order to enter His kingdom (Mark 1:15). Jesus devoted His earthly ministry to preaching the gospel of the kingdom (Mark 1:14; Matt. 4:23). After His resurrection, He devoted much of the forty days before His ascension to teaching His disciples about the kingdom of God (Acts 1:3).

Jesus was emphatic that advancing the coming of the kingdom required evangelism. He made being born again a requirement for entrance (John 3:3, 5). Later, in that same conversation, Jesus further clarified the issue when He told Nicodemus, "And as Moses lifted up the serpent in the wilderness, even so must the Son of Man be lifted up, that whoever believes in Him should not perish but have everlasting life" (John 3:14–15).

This emphasis of Jesus on getting people into His kingdom through evangelism cannot be omitted from any discussion of the interpretation of *Your kingdom come.* This evangelistic interpretation harmonizes with Jesus's stated reason for His incarnation. He stated, "For the Son of Man has come to seek and save the lost" (Luke 19:10). The lost were saved by becoming subjects of the King and being made citizens of His everlasting kingdom.

This evangelistic interpretation also harmonizes with His stated purpose of His church. He commands them to "Go therefore and make disciples of all the nations, baptizing them in the name of the Father and of the Son and of the Holy Spirit, teaching them to observe all things that I have commanded you; and lo, I am with you always, even to the end of the age. Amen" (Matt. 28:19–20).

This urgent prayer also anticipates the coming of the literal kingdom in all its power and glory. Believers are not to sink their roots too deeply in this world since they are just passing through down here. They are to live with one eye on earth and one on the horizon looking for the return of their Lord and the institution of His literal kingdom in all its power and glory.

The Phases of the Kingdom

As an everlasting kingdom (Ps. 145:13; Dan. 4:3), God's kingdom did not open its doors for business when John the Baptist and Jesus came preaching. "Repent for the Kingdom of Heaven is at hand" (Matt.

3:2, 4:17). According to Jesus, Abraham, Isaac, and Jacob were already citizens of His eternal kingdom. He affirmed this when He told the Roman centurion, "I say unto you that many will come from east and west, and recline at the table with Abraham, Isaac, and Jacob in the kingdom of heaven" (Matt. 8:11). John and Jesus were offering entrance into an everlasting kingdom that was already present in its first phase with two phases still future.

Phase 1

The first phase of the kingdom rule and authority of Jesus in the hearts of men began in the Garden at creation and lasts until His Second Advent to the earth at the end of the Great Tribulation. At that time, Jesus returns to defeat the antichrist and his vast hordes (Rev. 19:17–21) and set up His millennial kingdom (Rev. 20:1–6). For the church, this first phase ends at the Rapture when they are caught up to meet their Lord in the clouds to be with Him forever (1 Thess. 4:13–18).

During this first phase, the kingdom manifests itself primarily through the King's rule and authority in the hearts and lives of His born-again subjects (Matt. 7:21; Luke 17:21). They become subject to His kingdom rule and authority when they repent and believe and are born into His kingdom by the new birth (Mark 1:14–15; John 3:3, 5, 16, 18, 36). This makes them kingdom Christians.

Since Pentecost, God has chosen to work primarily through His church to advance the coming of His kingdom rule and authority in the hearts of the unsaved through evangelism. The biblical vision of every member of any local church needs to be "To know Him and make Him known from my house to the regions beyond."

Phase 2

The second phase of the kingdom begins after the defeat of the anti-christ (the beast) and his massive army at the battle of Armageddon (Rev. 19:19–21). After this major event, Jesus will establish His kingdom on this earth and rule and reign with His saints for a thousand years (Rev. 20:4–6). At the end of this thousand years, God frees the devil for a short season. He proceeds to amass a massive army of rebels who had rejected Christ's kingdom rule and authority during His thousand-year reign of peace and prosperity. The devil and his hordes are defeated and sealed forever in the lake of fire along with the antichrist, the false prophet, and all the unsaved (Rev. 20:7–10, 15). This concludes the second phase of the Kingdom which is followed by the Great White Throne Judgment of the lost (Rev. 20:11-15).

Phase 3

The third and final phase of the everlasting kingdom begins on the new earth and in the New Jerusalem (Rev. 21:22) immediately after the Great White Throne Judgment (Rev. 20:11–15). This final phase marks Jesus's complete recovery and restoration of everything Adam forfeited in his garden paradise at his fall. Phase 3 is the garden paradise restored to the Father's children but on a superior level where they will know God in an inviolable relationship as both their Creator and Redeemer.

Conclusion

The Christian world is now populated by inward focused denominational Christians instead of upward and outward focused Kingdom Christians. Denominationalism and selfism have fragmented and weakened the body of Christ's focus on advancing the coming of the Kingdom through personal and world evangelism. Kingdom Christianity is upward focused on Jesus and outward focused on the perishing souls of men.

Life Lessons
"YOUR KINGDOM COME"

God's kingdom is both a spiritual and a literal kingdom.

God's kingdom is a dynamic kingdom that is present but still coming.

God's kingdom can only be accessed by the new birth.

God's kingdom focuses on His rule and authority which is advanced by evangelism.

God's kingdom is populated by loving and loyal patriotic citizens.

GOD'S WORD REVEALS GOD'S WILL

GUIDE NO. 4

Praying and Living Guided by My Father's Will

Chapter 4

Prostrate before the Father

Your will be done on earth, as it is in heaven.
—*Matthew 6:10*

*Let it come to be, the will of you, as
in heaven, so also on earth.*
—*Literal translation*

Introduction: "God's Will Is a Big Deal!"

Jesus purposely placed His fourth guide, *Your will be done*, in the exact center of His seven guides on how believers are to think, pray, and live. It is in the center because God's sovereign authority is the central truth of the ages. This center guide ties Jesus's three preceding and succeeding guides together. None of the others work unless a person is willing to bow to the will or authority of God.[6] Nobody can know God as their Father or enter His kingdom until they bow to His will which is the expression of His authority. Saving faith is a faith which trusts in

---

[6] The form of the Greek word *ginomai* that is translated as "be done" is another aorist, passive, imperative, third person singular. As an imperative, it normally functions as a command. However, when addressed to God, it constitutes an urgent plea instead of a command. The literal translation is "Let Your will be done on earth as it is in heaven."

the character of a holy and loving God enough to bow to His will and submit one's entire life into His hands.

The eleven words, *Your will be done on earth, as it is in heaven*, are laden with far-reaching spiritual life-changing implications, some of which are given below:

First, God's will is the outward expression to man of Who He is in His innermost being.

Second, God's will is knowable.

Third, God's will is doable.

Fourth, God's will is comprehensive and binding.

Defining the Will of God

God's will is His outward expression to men on how He expects them to live based upon Who He is in the deepest recesses of His holy and loving being. Because His will is the outward expression of His inner holy and loving nature, it always functions for His glory and man's highest good.

God's first words to mankind in Genesis 1:1 are an assertion of His sovereign authority over His creation and creatures. His first words remind men that He created them and the world they live in. They are living on His earth, drinking His water, breathing His air, and eating His food. Their next breath, beat of their heart, and blink of their eyes come from Him. It is in Him that they live, move, and have their being (Acts 17:28). Therefore, He has the right to tell them how He wants them to think, pray, and live. The absolute authority of God over His creation and creatures is the core truth and the battleground of the ages.

God's will (authority) is always guided by His holy and loving nature. It is impossible for God to violate His holy and loving nature and will to do anything harmful to man, His highest and most treasured creation. God's outward actions toward men are always consistent with Who He is in the deepest recesses of His being. Jesus illustrates this concept by His declaration that the words of one's mouth reveal who he is in his heart or in the depths of his being. He told the Pharisees:

> Either make the tree good and its fruit good, or else make the tree bad and its fruit bad; for a tree is known by its fruit. Brood of vipers! How can you, being evil, speak good things? For out of the abundance of the heart the mouth speaks. A good man out of the good treasure [b]of his heart brings forth good things, and an evil man out of the evil treasure brings forth evil things. But I say to you that for every idle word men may speak, they will give account of it in the day of judgment. For by your words you will be justified, and by your words, you will be condemned. (Matt. 12:33–37)

When Jesus says that it is out of the abundance of the heart that the mouth speaks, He is saying that who a person is in his innermost being determines what he thinks, says, and does. Jesus then simplifies His statement by His declaration that a good man out of the good treasure of his heart brings forth good things and an evil man out of the evil treasure brings forth evil things. Thus, if a man is evil in the core of his being (heart), what he wills will also be evil. On the other hand, if he is good in the core of his being, what he wills will be good, and he will bring forth good fruit.

God's will is His personal resolve. His will is not a set of impersonal laws formulated by some insensitive impersonal legislative body. His will is His personal expression to men on how He expects them to live. This makes ignoring or disobeying God's will a personal offense, and He takes it seriously. Intelligent men should be apprehensive about offending the Lord God Almighty, Creator of the heavens and the earth, Who holds all humanity's next heartbeat in His hand.

God's will can be further defined as His *general will* for all men and His *specific will* for His children. His *general will* has to do with His moral requirements on all men as expressed in His divine moral code revealed in His Word and summarized in the Ten Commandments. His *specific will* has to do with the specific role He assigns each of His children in fulfilling the Great Commission. Each of His children is a unique creation with a unique role to perform in fulfilling the Great Commission. Others can fulfill that same role, but the unique personality of each of God's children means that nobody can do it exactly like them.

God's will is an expression of His love. His will is always designed for men's highest good. The center of God's will is the safest, the happiest, the most fulfilling, and the most rewarding place a believer can be. Success and failure in this life and at the judgment will be measured by conformity to the will of God. Every thought, motive, word, or deed of life needs to be measured by the holy and loving will of a holy and loving God.

Discerning the Will of God

Since God expects men to do His will, then His justice demands that His will must be both *knowable* and *doable*. A just God cannot hold men accountable for not doing what He has not made known to them;

neither can He hold them accountable for not doing that which is impossible for them to do. The holy and just nature of God dictates that He reveal to men what He wants them to do and then provide them the means of doing it.

God reveals His will primarily through His *Word, prayer,* and *the inner promptings of the still small voice of the Holy Spirit,* through *circumstances* and *godly counsel.* These are the most common ways God reveals Himself and His will to men. However, nobody can put God into his little theological box and tell Him how He must communicate His will. Variances from His established ways of communicating His will are rare and demand extreme caution. Just because a person says "God told me" does not mean God told him. Just because a person says he saw a vision from God does not mean it was from God. Everything must accord with the Scriptures.

Discerning God's specific will is more involved than discerning His general will which is clearly defined in His Word. However, although His specific will and calling is not clearly defined in His Word, it is knowable to those who desire to know and do His will. God is still capable of calling and putting His servants *exactly where* He wants them *exactly when* He wants them there.

Three Biblical Guides on Discerning God's Specific Will based upon Proverbs 3:5–6

Trust in the Lord with all your heart. People do not submit their lives and destiny into the hand of someone they do not trust. Neither will God reveal His will to those who do not trust Him. Discerning the specific will of God begins with trust.

Lean not on your understanding. There must come a time when the believer comes to the very end of any reliance on himself. He must learn to lean on God, His Word, the indwelling Holy Spirit, divine providence, and godly counsel to discern God's will.

In all your ways, acknowledge Him, and He will direct your paths. God does not do business with rebels. God gives discernment to those who surrender their entire life into His hands. God only reveals His will to those who are completely surrendered to His will.

Practical Observations on Discerning God's Specific Will

God reveals His specific will only to those who are doing His general will. One can never discern God's specific will while refusing to do what he already knows God wants him to do (John 7:17).

God's specific will always harmonizes with His Word. The Holy Spirit, Who inspired the authors to write God's Word, will never contradict Himself by leading anyone to violate what He led these men to write (Ps. 119:105).

God's specific will never contradict His holy and loving nature. Any thought, motive, or deed that violates God's holy and loving nature is never the will of God.

God's specific will is validated by God's ways. God's ways are as big as His will. Where He leads, He meets the needs; and where He guides, He provides (Rev. 3:8; Phil. 4:19).

Four Critical Questions in Discerning God's Specific Will

What would Jesus do if He were standing here? Sensing the mind of Christ is primarily determined by the intimacy of one's relationship with Him growing out of prayer, time in His Word, and His Holy Spirit anointing.

Will this violate God's holy and loving nature? Glorifying God's name as holy must be the measure of every thought, word, and deed of life. Believers win the respect of the world by being holy. They win the hearts of the world by being compassionate.

Will this advance or hinder the coming of the Father's kingdom rule and authority in the hearts of men through evangelism? The advancement of His kingdom takes priority over the desires of the flesh.

Will this violate the teachings of the Scriptures? Any contemplated action that violates the teachings of the Word of God is never the will of God. God never grants variances to what He said in His Word.

Doing the Will of God

A loving just God is never going to command His children to do His will and not provide them the motivation and the means to do it. God's children are not doomed to live defeated lives dominated by sin and their sinful nature. He tells them, "For sin shall not have dominion over you, for you are not under law but under grace" (Rom. 6:14). Saving grace is also a transforming grace (Titus 2:11–13).

Paul attributes doing the will of God to Christ and the Holy Spirit's divine enablement. He recognized his inability to do the will of God and wrote, "O wretched man that I am! Who will deliver me from this body of death?" Thanks be to God through Jesus Christ our Lord (Rom. 7:24–25)! The apostle did not attribute his victory over sin and doing the will of God to any secret formula he had found within himself. He recognized that he was not able to grit his teeth, stiffen his back, bow his neck, and subdue his flesh and do the will of God. Paul describes the moral corruption of his flesh in the following manner, "In my flesh dwells no good thing" (7:18). Victory over the flesh only comes *through Jesus Christ our Lord and His Holy Spirit anointing.*

No believer will see his need to begin looking to Christ and *walking after the spirit* in Romans chapter 8 without first coming to the very end of himself in chapter 7 and crying out, "O wretched man that I am, who can deliver me from this body of death?" Then and only then will he humbly cast himself totally upon Jesus, His Word, and His Holy Spirit anointing to enable him to subdue his flesh. Then the righteous requirement of the law can be fulfilled in us who do not walk according to the flesh but according to the Spirit (Rm. 8:4).

The Bible attributes doing the will of God to loving God and having a healthy respectful fear of Him. There is an inseparable relationship between one's attitude toward God and his attitude toward doing His will. The book of Proverbs declares, "By the fear of the Lord men depart from evil" (Prov. 16:6). In explaining his indictment of all men as sinners in Romans chapter 3, Paul attributes their appetite for sin to the fact that "there is no fear of God before their eyes" (Rom. 3:18). A fearful reverence for God expresses itself in doing His will. The two are inseparable.

"The love for God implanted by the Holy Spirit in the heart of God's children at conversion motivates them to do His will" (Rom. 5:5). Love always seeks to please the one who is loved. This supernaturally implanted love for God moves His children to seek to please their Father by doing His will (John 14:21).

The justice of God motivates His children to do His will. The justice of God dictates that every sin has consequences (Gal. 6:7–8). There are no free sins. Every sin has consequences in this life and eternity. The substitutionary atoning death of Christ does void the death penalty of sin for believers, but it does not void the consequences of sin in this life or the loss of rewards in eternity.

"God's love for His children motivates them to do His will" (Gal. 6:9–10). It is much more desirable to obey a loving God than a harsh legalistic god. It is much easier to obey a loving God Who always seeks to do what is best for you and to bless your life than to obey someone who seeks to do you harm. Doing His will is not always convenient or pleasant, but even when it is painful, it is always made easier by His unfailing love.

The rewards for doing God's will motivate the Father's children to do His will. The center of God's will is the safest, most fulfilling, most exciting, and most rewarding place a believer can be in this life. However, there is coming a great payday in the skies when God will give eternal rewards to each of His children based on their faithfulness in doing His will on earth.

Faith in God is the strongest motivation for doing His will. Nobody is going to submit his life into the hands of a person he does not trust. A person's faith in God determines the depths of his submission to doing His will. This kind of faith can say to God, "Father, I do not understand or like what You are doing in my life. However, because I know that You love me and will never make a mistake and You will always do what is right and best for Your glory and my good, I gladly submit my life into Your hands."

Doing All the Will of God All the Time

As a continuous action command, the form of the Greek verb translated as "be done" means that God expects men to do all His will all the time. God's strong condemnation of Saul's "pick-and-choose" obedience to His will in his refusal to kill King Agag and his choice livestock dictates that doing all His will all the time is extremely important to God (1 Sam. 15:2–23).

There is a dangerous and growing misconception in the carnal American church that much of the will of God is optional. God's will is not God's suggestions. His will is not a "pick-and-choose" will. Christianity is not a smorgasbord religion. One of the very best measures of one's attitude toward God is his attitude toward His will. Irreverence toward His will grows out of an irreverence toward God. Dedication to God is primarily expressed by a dedication to doing all His will all the time.

The command that men do His will on earth as in heaven, where it is done perfectly, makes God's will both comprehensive *and* binding. God's will is never optional. Nothing and nobody is beyond the scope of His will. Christians tend to create a condescending order of the importance of God's will. They place a few things at the top of their priority list as things God expects them to do or not do. The further down on their list things appear, the less important doing those things becomes. It appears that some believers think that they have the authority to deem some things beyond the scope of God's will and authority.

Conclusion

The will or the sovereign authority of God goes to the core of both Bible Christianity and human existence. All of God's creation and creatures exist only by His sovereign will. Residence in heaven or hell is determined by one's response to the will of God. Success in this life and eternity is determined by one's response to the will of God. God's will is a big deal!

Life Lessons

"YOUR WILL BE DONE"

The will of God is His inner resolve on how He wants men to think, pray, and live.

The will of God is Who He is in His innermost being.

The will of God is the expression of His holy and loving nature.

The will of God is designed for His glory and man's highest good.

The will of God is comprehensive, inevitable, and invincible.

THE BELIEVER'S
INEXHAUSTIBLE RESOURCE

GUIDE NO. 5

Totally Dependent upon My Father for:
My Next Biscuit
My Next Breath
My Next Beat of My Heart
My Next Blink of My Eye

Chapter 5

The Provisions of the Father

Give us this day our daily bread.
—Matthew 6:11

The bread of us daily, You give to us today.
—Literal translation

Introduction

People are much more prone to pray for their daily bread when they constantly struggle for food. People with full refrigerators and freezers and ready access to a grocery store with shelves lined with food are far less likely to pray for their daily bread. This guide is given by Jesus as a constant reminder of the proud hearts of men that it is still God Who stocks the shelves at the grocery store and in their homes. The proud heart is prone to assert its independence from God as is indicated in the following passage:

> Otherwise, you may say in your heart, "My power and the strength of my hand made me this wealth." But you shall remember the LORD your God, for it is He who is giving you the power to make

wealth, which He may confirm His covenant which He swore to your fathers, as it is this day. (Deut. 8:17–18)

This command for believers to pray daily for their sustenance is a divine call from God to His children for the following:

- A divine call for daily fellowship
- A divine call for a daily dose of humility and gratitude
- A divine call for a daily dose of moderation
- A divine call for a daily dose of compassion
- A divine call for a daily strengthening of faith that relieves one of undue anxiety

A Daily Call for Fellowship

One of the most amazing truths about the God of the Bible is the fact that He created man in His image as His highest and most treasured creation for His fellowship. This guide to daily call on the Father for one's supply of bread is also the call of a loving Father Who hungers for fellowship with His children. That is an explosive truth!

There are three great acts of God which prove the intensity of His earnest desire for fellowship with man. First, the fact that God created man in His image as a social being capable of fellowship with Him testifies to His desire for fellowship with man (Gen. 1:26–27).

Second, heaven is striking testimony of God's intense desire for eternal and unbroken fellowship with His redeemed children (Rev. 21:3–4). Third, Calvary is the ultimate testimony of God's intense desire for fellowship with man (Jn. 3:16). Only the Christian God would sacrifice His Son on Calvary to make possible the restoration of His broken fellowship with man.

Jesus gave this command to pray daily for bread for several reasons, and one of them is to create another avenue of daily fellowship between a loving Father and His children.

A Daily Dose of Humility and Gratitude

The great Babylonian king, Nebuchadnezzar, stood gazing on the great city of Babylon and could not restrain his pride and boasted, "Is this not great Babylon, that I have built for a royal dwelling by my mighty power and for the honor of my majesty?" (Dan. 4:30). God responded by removing him from his exalted position and humbled him to live as an animal. After seven years, this proud king came to realize "that the most High rules in the kingdom of men and gives it to whomever He chooses" (Dan. 4:32). Nebuchadnezzar was humbled by God to teach him one of the great lessons of life. It is God Who determines the failure and success of all men, great or small.

The Apostle Paul reminded the intelligentsia on Mars Hill in Athens that he was introducing them to their "unknown God." In his introduction of the real God, Paul reminded these polytheists that the real God is the Creator of all things (Acts 17:24). Then he reminded them that they were dependent upon Him for their existence. In verse 25, Paul told them that this Creator God *gives to all life, breath, and all things.* Later, he would tell them that "in Him we live and move and have our being" (Acts 17:25, 28). This daily prayer for bread is given by Jesus as a daily taste of humble pie for the proud heart of man.

Pride is self-dependence, while humility is God dependence. Pride is the root of all sin. The middle letter of both pride and sin is the letter "I." Pride causes the world to revolve around "me," while humility causes the world to revolve around God. His grace is on the humble, and His wrath is on the proud. The proud are banished to hell, and the humble inherit the earth (Matt. 5:5).

Humility is neither weakness nor timidity. Humility is not groveling, and neither is it a sign of low self-esteem. The following passages demonstrate God's requirement for humility and the value He places on humility:

> He has shown you, O man, what is good, and what the Lord requires of you, but to do justly and to love mercy, and to *walk humbly* with your God. (Mic. 6:8)

> Humble yourselves in the sight of the Lord, and he will lift you up. (James 4:10)

> If my people, who are called by my name, *will humble themselves* and pray and seek my face and turn from their wicked ways, then I will hear from heaven, and I will forgive their sin and will heal their land. (2 Chron. 7:14)

> …The greatest among you will be your servant. Whoever exalts himself will be humbled, and whoever humbles himself will be exalted. (Matt. 23:11–12)

> …God resists the proud but gives grace to the humble. (James 4:6)

This guide was never intended to inform an omniscient God of one's daily needs. God already knows what His children need before they ask (Matt. 6:8). Jesus's fifth guide is designed as a daily reminder to man of his helpless and hopeless state and to humble him and create in him an attitude of gratitude. God places a premium on a thankful heart because genuine thankfulness can only germinate and grow in a humble heart.

A Daily Dose of Moderation

This command to pray for one's daily needs was also a daily call for moderation. Jesus did not urge believers to pray for the essentials necessary to supply them for a week, a month, or a year because they needed to learn the critical lesson of moderation by trusting God on a daily basis for their needs.

Excess is the mother of pride and the enemy of faith. It feeds the insatiable appetite of the flesh and diminishes the appetite for sacrifice. Moderation keeps one humble and on his knees. Moderation dictates the self-discipline to restrain one's appetite. Moderation strengthens faith as God meets one's needs daily.

Moderation is not a call to poverty. Jesus never makes poverty a sign of spirituality. His call to moderation is a call to a balanced Christian life that keeps Jesus as the first love and loyalty of life. It is a warning of the dangers of excess whether it be bread or money. The author of Proverbs had moderation in mind when he wrote, "Give me neither poverty nor riches; feed me with the food that is needful for me, lest I be full and deny you and say, 'Who is the LORD?' or lest I be poor and steal and profane the name of my God" (Prov. 30:8–9).

A Daily Dose of Compassion

Jesus never uses the first person singular pronouns "I," "me," and "my" in His seven guides. By divine design, He did not direct believers to ask their heavenly Father to give "me" today "my" daily bread. Jesus was aware of the selfish inclinations of the depraved heart, even the hearts of His regenerate children. He used these plural personal pronouns to keep His children from becoming too inward focused and create a balance between self and others. This demand to also pray for "our" daily bread provides a much needed daily dose of genuine Christian compassion for others.

These plural forms do not mean that Christians are not to pray for their personal needs. After all, Jesus prayed in the garden, "Father, if it is your will, remove this cup from ME" (Luke 22:42). It is a matter of balance. Jesus used these plural forms to remind Christians of their need to guard against the natural inclinations of their fallen hearts to pray selfishly. Selfish prayer is wasted prayer. Christians do have a natural concern for their daily bread, but Jesus uses these plural forms to help keep them both inward and outward focused. They must also have a concern for the daily bread of others.

The focus of one's prayers is the barometer of the focus of their life. (This is true of both individuals and churches.) The driving force behind the church's compassion for the hurting and needy must always be their greater compassion for their spiritual needs. A hungry man does need bread, but his greatest need is the Bread of Life. It is a sin not to give him physical bread, but it is a greater sin to give him physical bread and not offer him the Bread of Life.

A Daily Dose of Faith That Reduces Anxiety

After the fall, man's life revolves around his constant struggle for food, shelter, and clothing. These daily necessities are summed up with the term "bread." They are inescapable realities of life. They begin early in life and haunt every member of Adam's race until death. Survival in a sin-cursed world drives some to commit the most heinous of crimes to guarantee the necessities of life.

There is an inescapable anxiety in the heart of man over future needs. Jesus was speaking to this strategic issue when He urged believers to come to their loving Father daily trusting in Him to supply their daily needs. His instruction to pray, *Give us this day our daily bread*, communicates three great truths which can deliver His children from the undue anxiety of future food, shelter, and clothing.

The Father is concerned for the daily welfare of each of His children. He is saying, "If you come to Me daily trusting Me for your daily needs, I will meet them because I care for every detail of your life." Peter admonishes believers to "cast all your cares upon Him, for He cares for you" (1 Pet. 5:7).

In the same chapter where He instructed believers to pray and ask the Father to *give us today our daily bread*, Jesus goes into detail in giving arguments to alleviate the Father's children from being overly concerned about their daily needs. In the following passage, Jesus gives three truths about the Father that should lay to rest any undue anxiety over one's daily needs:

> "Therefore I say to you, do not worry about your
> life, what you will eat or what you will drink; nor
> about your body, what you will put on. Is not life

more than food and the body more than clothing? Look at the birds of the air, for they neither sow nor reap nor gather into barns; yet your heavenly Father feeds them. Are you not of more value than they? Which of you by worrying can add one [a] cubit to his [b]stature?

So why do you worry about clothing? Consider the lilies of the field, how they grow: they neither toil nor spin; and yet I say to you that even Solomon in all his glory was not [c]arrayed like one of these. Now if God so clothes the grass of the field, which today is, and tomorrow is thrown into the oven, *will He* not much more *clothe* you, O you of little faith?

Therefore do not worry, saying, 'What shall we eat?' or 'What shall we drink?' or 'What shall we wear?' For after all these things the Gentiles seek. For your heavenly Father knows that you need all these things. But seek first the kingdom of God and His righteousness, and all these things shall be added to you." (Matt. 6:25–33).

First, He argues from the "lesser to the greater" by comparing man, God's highest and most treasured creation, with birds and the lilies of the field. He reasons that if their Father takes care of the birds and the flowers, He will obviously take care of His children. Second, He argues that they do not need to be overly concerned about their daily needs because their heavenly Father is always aware of their needs. He reminds believers, "For your heavenly Father knows that you need all these things." They do not ask Him for their daily bread because

He needs to be reminded of their need. They need to ask Him daily because *they* need to be reminded daily of Who supplies their needs.

Finally, Jesus seeks to refocus their concerns to a higher cause than self. He promises that if they make the pursuit of the kingdom of God and His righteousness their priority, the Father would take care of their daily needs or "these things." Jesus expressed this promise as follows, "But seek first the kingdom of God and His righteousness, and all these things shall be added to you" (Matt. 6:33). Jesus argues that if believers put God first in their lives, He will take care of them.

His supply is limitless, and He promises, "My Father shall supply all your needs according to His riches in glory by Christ Jesus" (Phil. 4:19). Jesus draws this bountiful supply from His endless riches which can never be exhausted (Phil. 4:19). Their heavenly Father is never going to run out of food, clothing, and shelter in this world nor paradise to come. His children never need fear about the future. Their heavenly Father has an inexhaustible supply that will last for all eternity.

The Apostle Paul wrote, "Be careful for nothing *[do not worry about anything]*; but in everything, by prayer and supplication with thanksgiving, let your requests be made known unto God" (Phil. 4:6). Later he wrote, "…But my God shall supply all your need according to his riches in glory by Christ Jesus" (Phil. 4:19). Undue anxiety over food, clothing, and shelter is a sin against the Father Who has pledged His sacred honor to look after His children.

Worry is an act of unbelief. It is to doubt God's integrity. Doubt and worry inhibit true worship and praise. They shift one's focus from God to self. This fifth guide is designed to daily focus one's faith on God in reliance upon Him to keep His Word.

I was in class working on my doctorate at Liberty Baptist Theological Seminary the week that Dr. Jerry Falwell died. His long-time friend and associate, Dr. Elmer Towns, taught the class. During the week, Dr. Towns shared several insights into the heart of this visionary man of faith. One of those glimpses was a very moving story about a short, powerful prayer that Dr. Falwell prayed during one of the many financial struggles in the early days of what would become Liberty University.

The college was under great financial stress; and Dr. Falwell, who was a man of great faith, called off classes for a day of prayer. The faculty and student body met for prayer, and then Dr. Falwell led them to march around one of the new buildings that stood unfinished due to lack of funds. They marched around the building and knelt to pray. Dr. Towns knelt beside his friend Dr. Falwell, and they prayed together.

Dr. Towns related only one sentence of Dr. Falwell's prayer, but it is one of the most moving short prayers this author has ever heard or read, and he has read many of the classics on prayer. Dr. Falwell made the following short and simple request that day, but it speaks volumes about this visionary's great faith and his intimate walk with his God. Here is what Dr. Jerry Falwell prayed, "Dear Lord, You have plenty of money, and I know it, and I need some of it."

The language of this prayer is the language of a deep faith growing out of an intimate relationship with his Father. It is not the formal language of asking a favor from a casual acquaintance. This short prayer is the language of a friend speaking to a trusted friend he knows and trusts so well that he can be completely open and honest with Him. It is the language of intimacy that can exist only between two close and dear friends.

It exuberates with complete honesty that says "I am broke, but I know that you have plenty of money." The statement "And I need some of it" exuberates with a sense of expectancy that he expects his trusted friend to give him some of His bountiful supply of money. Dr. Jerry Falwell was a visionary, and nobody's vision ever exceeds his faith. His great faith grew out of his intimate relationship with his Lord that was created by time alone with Him in prayer and in His Word.

The number 1 priority of this guide, *Give us today our daily bread*, is a call to daily fellowship that will intensify one's relationship with his heavenly Father that results in a faith that alleviates anxiety over daily needs.

Life Lessons
"GIVE US THIS DAY OUR DAILY BREAD"

Daily prayer for daily bread is an expression of God's intense desire for daily fellowship with His children.

Prayer for daily bread is a daily reminder of the Father's loving concern for the lives of His children.

Daily prayer for daily bread is a daily dose of gratitude and humility.

Prayer for daily bread is a daily reminder of one's total dependence upon his heavenly Father.

Daily prayer for daily bread increases faith and reduces anxiety.

A Brief Introduction to Jesus's Final Two Guides

A casual reading of Jesus's first five guides would leave one a bit baffled that a holy God did not boldly confront the critical sin issue early in His instructions on how believers are to pray and live. However, a close analysis of these guides will reveal that each of the first five does confront sin. First, before one can qualify to address God as his heavenly Father, he must first be born into His family by the new birth. The new birth requires repentance of sin and faith in Jesus and His redemptive sacrifice before gaining access into His kingdom (Mark 1:15).

Second, nobody can glorify the name of God as holy apart from confronting sin in their life. Unholy people cannot hallow the Father's name as holy. Third, advancing the coming of the kingdom through evangelism demands that lost sinners be confronted about sin and their need to repent. Fourth, nobody can be serious about doing the will of God apart from obeying His command to be holy (1 Pet. 1:15–16). Fifth, prayer for one's daily bread requires confession of sin because God does not hear the prayers of those who regard iniquity in their hearts (Ps. 66:18).

In His sixth guide, Jesus boldly confronts sin in the lives of believers by instructing them to seek forgiveness and cleansing of their sins. He then demands that they be compassionate people by forgiving those who sin against them.

In His seventh guide, Jesus again boldly confronts sin by giving God's plan on how to face and overcome the temptations of the evil one to sin. He offers divine direction and deliverance to those who turn to Him in earnest prayer.

These final two guides reveal a loving Father reaching out to His children to make them holy because holiness brings His blessings, their happiness, and His Holy Spirit anointing on their lives.

God never takes sin lightly. In some manner, Jesus confronts sin in each of His seven guides on how to pray effectively and live a fruitful Christian life. However, in His two final guides, Jesus boldly confronts sin and explains how Christians can be forgiven, overcome temptations to sin, and live a victorious Christian life.

FORGIVENESS DOES NOT APPROVE OR EXCUSE SIN

GUIDE NO. 6

Praying and Living as Forgiven While Forgiving Others

FORGIVENESS IS GOD'S *DIVINE* WASHING POWDER
GOD USES CLEAN VESSELS
THE FORGIVEN FORGIVE
GOD ANOINTS THE FORGIVEN WHO FORGIVE

Chapter 6

The Purging of the Father

And forgive us our debts, as we forgive our debtors.
—Matthew 6:12

And forgive us the debts of us, as we
have already forgiven our debtors.
—Literal translation

Introduction

This guide is primarily about healing fractured relationships caused by sin. It is first and foremost about reconciling God and man. Second, it is about reconciling man with his fellow man. This guide grows out of God's intense desire for an intimate personal relationship with His children and His desire that they maintain intimate relationships with each other. It confronts the most dangerous and deadly enemy known to man. This guide offers the only cure for the deadly curse of sin.

Apart from this prayer, *Forgive us our debts as we forgive our debtors,* there is no cure for the curse of sin that defiles and dooms humanity. God holds the patent on the only supernatural medicine that can cure the curse of sin. Only the Great Physician is authorized to dispense His patented cure. It can only be obtained free of charge at the dispensary of grace, but it was manufactured at an infinite cost on a hill called Calvary. The cure guarantees healing that lasts forever.

The cure of the Great Physician restores broken relationships between a man and his God and with his fellow man. This divine reconciliation is essential to a civilized society and all interpersonal relationships. Being forgiven and forgiving others is critical to one's happiness and his emotional and physical health. Forgiveness restores broken relationships, but it also restores broken lives.

Divine forgiveness is not defined or measured by human forgiveness. Human forgiveness must be defined and measured by divine forgiveness as revealed in God's Word. Given below are some truths drawn from Jesus's instruction to pray, *Forgive us our debts, as we forgive our debtors*:

- Divine Justice demands Divine Forgiveness
- A satanic deception about divine forgiveness
- A divine deduction that the forgiven forgive

Divine Justice Demands Divine Forgiveness

God's holiness demanded Calvary. His love provided Calvary. The center cross on Calvary's brow almost two thousand years ago stands as the world's most outstanding testimony of holiness and love known to man. Calvary also stands as the greatest legal transaction known to man since it balanced the books of God's justice in the courts of heaven. The substitutionary, sacrificial, atoning death of the Son of God made it possible for God to forgive guilty sinners and maintain His justice. This explains Paul's reference to Him as the "Just Justifier" (Rom. 3:26).

The literal meaning of the Greek word translated as forgiveness is to remit, release, send away, cancel, pardon, or remove the guilt and punishment of wrongdoing. When used in the New Testament regarding God's divine forgiveness of the penitent believing sinner, the word takes on a much deeper theological meaning.

A Definition of Divine Forgiveness

Forgiveness is the free act of a sovereign merciful God as He reaches out in grace offering complete reconciliation to guilty, condemned sinners who repent and believe. Repentance involves a deep sense of guilt and sorrow for sin that leads sinners to turn in faith to Christ trusting in His redemptive work on Calvary as full and final payment for their sins. When an individual repents and believes, God graciously removes the guilt and punishment of all past, present, and future sins. He then restores him to full favor and views him as innocent of all charges and treats him as if the offense never occurred.

A Discussion of Divine Forgiveness

1. *Divine forgiveness is not a pardon in the traditional sense of the word.* A traditional human pardon voids the penalty of an offense and sets the offender free, but his crime goes unpunished. The authority figure voids the just punishment for the crimes of those he pardons. Voiding the just punishment for the guilty sinner never happens with a divine pardon. Divine justice dictates just punishment for every offense of God's holy law. Anything less would violate God's infinitely just nature.

   Therefore, divine forgiveness is not a pardon as understood in today's culture. When God pardons, He does not void the sinner's infinite sin-debt. He pardons the guilty sinner who repents and believes based upon the fact that his sin-debt has been paid in full by his substitute on Calvary.

2. *Divine forgiveness is conditioned upon repentance and faith.* Jesus made both repentance and believing necessary for salvation when He declared, "The time is fulfilled, and the kingdom of God is at hand. *Repent* and *believe* in the Gospel" (Mark 1:15). Repentance and faith are inseparable twins in that they are two aspects of the same event. It is impossible to repent in the biblical sense without believing. It is also impossible to believe without repenting. They are opposite sides of the same coin. As rain assumes water, repentance and faith assume each other.

    There are places in the New Testament that demand repentance without faith as the condition for forgiveness and salvation. There are even more places that demand faith without any mention of repentance as the condition of forgiveness and salvation. However, a comparison of these and other related passages reveals that when an inspired author uses one of these terms, he assumes the presence of the other since the two are inseparable.

    Paul told the Philippian jailer that he needed to believe to be saved (Acts 16:31). Peter stated that the Lord desires that all men repent and avoid perishing (2 Pet. 3:9). In Luke 13:3, Jesus declares that unless you repent, you will all likewise perish. In John 3:16, He declares that unless you believe, you will perish. In each of these instances, a part is used to stand for the whole.

    Paul used the terms in this manner when he told the Athenian intellectuals that God required all men to repent, but he then stated that some joined him and believed (Acts 17:30, 34). He told the Ephesian elders, "I did not shrink from declaring to you anything that was profitable...testifying both to Jews and to Greeks of *repentance* toward God and of *faith* in our Lord Jesus Christ" (Acts 20:20–21).

This statement affirms Paul's belief that these two terms describe a single act. Repentance is the recognition of one's guilt and condemnation because of his sins. Faith is the recognition that Jesus Christ and His redemptive work on Calvary is the only solution to his helpless condition. Sometimes a New Testament author will use one assuming the other, but occasionally he will use both terms referring to the same event of being forgiven and saved.

3. *Divine forgiveness involves the critical doctrine of imputation.*
    The Greek word Jesus used for "forgive" is *aphiemi*. It has the basic meaning of "release, send away, cancel, remit, pardon, or remove the guilt and punishment of wrongdoing." When applied to the repentant sinner who turns in faith to Christ, God transfers the sinner's guilt to His Son (Isa. 53:4–6, 1 Pet. 3:18, 2 Cor. 5:21). He also transfers His Son's sin-payment to the guilty sinner (Rom. 3:24). This transfer of the sinner's guilt to Christ and Christ's redemptive work to the penitent sinner is called the doctrine of imputation.

Imputation also includes the guilty sinner being clothed in Christ's perfect obedience when he repents and believes. In the courts of heaven, Christ's perfect obedience to the holy law of God while incarnate is imputed to the believer's account when he repents and believes. When this happens, God then views him through the perfect righteousness of

Christ. God then views the forgiven sinner as innocent of all charges and treats him as if he had never sinned. The born-again believer stands fully accepted and loved by his heavenly Father based on the imputed merits of his Lord and Savior (Phil 3:9; Rom. 3:22).

4. *Divine forgiveness involves full payment of the guilty sinner's sin-debt.* When Jesus instructed believers to pray, *Forgive us our debts as we forgive our debtors*, the Greek word He used for "debts" was *opheilema*. When used literally, the word had to do with an individual who owed someone money. However, in rabbinic literature, it became the standard expression for indebtedness to God or to other humans. Jesus used this word "debt" to communicate the critical truth that sin incurs a debt that sinners owe God.

Man, who is a finite being, sinned against God, who is an infinite being. Therefore, man owes an infinite debt which, as a finite being, he can never pay. Only Jesus, as the infinite Son of God incarnated in a human body, could qualify as his substitute and pay his infinite sin-debt in full.

This infinite sin-debt explains why the Father rejected Jesus's plea in the garden, "Father, if there be any other way, let this cup pass from me" (Matt. 26:39). The only possible payment for man's infinite sin-debt was the substitutionary sacrificial sufferings and death of the infinite Son of God on Calvary's cross.

This fact explains Jesus's shout from the cross, *Tetelesthai*, which is translated, *It is finished.* However, this word could have also been translated *paid in full* (Matt. 27:50; John 19:30). The word was a commercial term in Christ's day.

When a debt was paid in full, the creditor often wrote the word *tetelesthai* across the bottom of the certificate of credit. He used this word to denote that the debtor had completed the payment of his debt and his debt was paid it in full. Jesus did both on Calvary. He brought the sin-debt owed by man to its completion because He had paid its penalty in full.

Man can add nothing to the finished work of Christ on Calvary. That person who repents and believes has his sin-debt paid in full by the sacrificial sufferings and death of his Lord on Calvary. Forgiveness is exclusively a work of God's amazing grace. It is as the poet wrote, "In my hand no price I bring; simply to the cross I cling."

A Satanic Deception about Divine Forgiveness

Satan has distorted God's gracious offer of forgiveness into an open license to sin. In the minds of millions, he has successfully distorted God's amazing grace into a disgrace. Satan has deceived them into thinking that they can commit a sin, bow their head, and ask God to forgive them and there are no further consequences of their sin. This lax view of the consequences of sin reflects a tragic misconception of the threefold curse of sin as well as the extent of divine forgiveness.

Sin incurs a threefold curse. Sin has a *time curse*, *eternity curse*, and *death curse*. Like the wake trailing behind a boat speeding across a placid lake, sin automatically brings in its wake this threefold curse. God does not personally dispatch these three curses when an individual sins. They are innate to every sin. Nobody ever needs to sue to collect the wages of sin. The three curses of sin which are explained below are innate to every sin and automatically accompany every sin.

Temporal Curse

This curse deals with the tragic effects of sin in this life or in time. God's justice includes an unalterable law of sowing and reaping in this life (Gal. 6:7–8). The Bible is replete with instances that prove that repentance and forgiveness *do not* negate the tragic consequences of sin in this life. There are no free sins. Every sin has its payday in this life as well as in eternity.

For example, David committed adultery with Bathsheba and had her husband murdered. Later, he repented in bitter tears, and God forgave him (Ps. 51); but for the rest of his life, David lived with the tragic consequences of his sins. Nathan the prophet told David that as a consequence of his sins of murder and adultery, the sword would never leave his house (2 Sam. 12:9-12). The prophet of God was reminding David that God is not mocked. The birds do come home to roost in this life as well as well as in eternity.

David had laid with Bathsheba, Uriah's wife, on the rooftop of his palace. His son, Absalom, would lie with his wives on that same rooftop of his palace. He had murdered Bathsheba's husband, Uriah the Hittite, and he lived to see four of his sons murdered before he died. Sin reaps its tragic harvest in this life. There are no free sins.[7]

The persecution and martyrdom of Paul illustrate this same temporal curse of sin. Before his conversion, Paul had viciously persecuted and

---

[7] First, the son born out of his illicit affair with Bathsheba died at birth. Second, David's son, Absalom, murdered another of his sons, Amnon, for raping Tamar his half-sister who was Absalom's full sister. Years later, David would endure the agony of Absalom's death in battle as he tried to usurp David's throne. Finally, he would witness the agony of Solomon having had his son Adonijah killed because he sought to seize the throne just prior to David's death (1 Kings 2:24–25). David pronounced a four-fold curse upon the wealthy man who took the poor man's ewe lamb. He reaped this four-fold curse in the death of four of his sons.

killed Christians. After being converted and forgiven on the Damascus Road, Paul was persecuted his entire ministry and eventually martyred in Rome at the hands of wicked Nero. Forgiveness does not void the curse of sin in this life.

Converted alcoholics continue to suffer the ravages of alcohol on their bodies although they have been forgiven. Forgiven drug addicts continue to suffer the ravages of drugs on their bodies, minds, emotions, and families. Those who have experienced God's gracious forgiveness from a life of promiscuity still suffer the ravages of social diseases contracted before being converted. There needs to be a renewed fear of a holy and loving God Who still punishes sin.

If this truth were more widely understood, there would be a greater fear of God Who punishes sin. God's inevitable law of sowing and reaping in this life and eternity is still in effect. Paul's warning should be painted on the billboard of every heart: "Be not deceived, God is not mocked, for whatsoever a man sows, that shall he also reap" (Gal. 6:7). Although God does not collect an "eye-for-an-eye" and a "tooth-for-a-tooth," He always punishes sin.

Eternal Curse

The eternal curse of sin has to do with the loss of eternal rewards in heaven for believers or the degree of punishment in hell for unbelievers based upon deeds committed in this life. After death, both the saved and the unsaved will stand before God in judgment. The saved will stand before the judgment seat of Christ (2 Cor. 5:10). A thousand years later, the unsaved will stand before the Great White Throne Judgment (Rev. 20:11–15). Both will be judged "according to their works or the deeds done in the body" (Rev. 20:12–13, 2 Cor. 5:10). John warns the unsaved that God has a record of their lives *written in the books* and each one will be judged *according to his works* (Rev. 20:11–12).

These passages prove that there will be degrees of rewards in heaven as well as degrees of punishment in hell. The justice of God dictates that forgiveness does not void the eternal consequences of sin in eternity. The repeated use of the words *according to* means that the rewards of the righteous in heaven are determined by their righteous deeds while on earth. These same two words also apply to the unsaved. The intensity of God's punishment in hell will also be determined by the intensity of their evil deeds in this life.

Sin does not sever a believer's relationship with his Lord, but it does diminish his effectiveness in the work of the Lord. Diminished effectiveness in this life diminishes one's rewards in eternity. The intensity of the evil deeds in the life of an unbeliever determines the intensity of his punishment in hell. Forgiveness does not alter the eternal curse of sin. If a believer steals God's tithe on earth, he will diminish his eternal rewards in Heaven. The greater the sins in the life of the unbeliever, the greater will be his punishment in Hell.

Death Curse

The Bible mentions two distinct death curses as the penalty of sin. Sin incurs the curse or penalty of *physical death* (Gen. 2:16–17; Rom. 6:23). Sin also incurs the penalty of the *second death* which is being cast into the lake of fire forever (Rev. 20:15, 21:8). The unforgiven suffer both these penalties. They die physically, but they are also cast into the lake of fire which is the second death penalty for sin (Rev. 20:14–15, 21:8).

Christians do suffer the physical death penalty of their sins since all Christians die. However, Jesus has already suffered the second death curse of their sins when He bore their hell for them on the cross. Therefore, divine forgiveness voids the second death curse of sin for those who repent and believe in the gospel. This second death curse of sin is the only part of the threefold curse of sin that is voided by divine forgiveness.

The modern church desperately needs to take a more serious view of sin and its tragic consequences. Modern Christianity needs to avoid turning grace into disgrace. God's gracious forgiveness is never a license to sin. Divine forgiveness does deliver believers from the second death curse of sin, but it does not void the tragic consequences of sin in this life and its diminishing of one's eternal rewards in heaven. Once again, there are no free sins.

A Divine Demand That the Forgiven Forgive

A casual reading of Jesus's statement "But if you do not forgive men their trespasses, neither will your Father forgive your trespasses" initially appears to make forgiving others conditional to being saved. However, Jesus is speaking to His disciples who are believers. Therefore, He is not urging saved people to forgive others as a condition to being saved. Instead, Jesus is warning believers that if they do not forgive others and restore them to fellowship, neither will their heavenly Father forgive and restore them to full fellowship.

No one is more Christlike than when he models before a watching world the example of a forgiving spirit. On the other hand, no one is less like Christ than when he harbors a bitter, unforgiving attitude toward his fellow man. It is impossible to be in proper fellowship with the Father while being out of fellowship with one's fellow man. Jesus is warning believers not to come to their heavenly Father seeking His fellowship and answers to their prayers while they are harboring the bitter poison of an unforgiving spirit in their heart.

Jesus is demanding complete openness and honesty in the relationship between believers and God. He is declaring that it is impossible to be out of fellowship with other believers and be in fellowship with God. Thus, if a believer is out of fellowship with others, he is also out of fellowship with his heavenly Father. Therefore, the starting point in being reconciled to the Father is being reconciled to others. There can be no deceit. Every root of bitterness must be rooted out. Forgiveness must be complete. Reconciliation must be real. Only when this forgiving mind and heart of Christ becomes real can one be restored to fellowship with his heavenly Father.

The Tragic Cost of an Unforgiving Heart

One of the most dangerous things a believer can do to himself, his family, his friends, and the cause of Christ is to harbor an unforgiving, bitter spirit. Refusal to forgive begins as a small kernel of bitterness in a proud heart that will gradually create a vindictive spirit that opens the door to unimaginable evil. This explains why the Bible admonishes believers not to let the sun go down on their wrath (Eph. 4:26).

The person who is bitter is often resentful, cynical, harsh, cold, relentless, and unpleasant to be around. Hebrews 12:15 warns, "See to it that no one misses the grace of God and that no bitter root grows up to cause trouble and defile many." The phrase *grows up* suggests bitterness's ability to spread and contaminate. The phrase *to cause trouble and defile many* serves as a divine warning of the contagious nature of bitterness and its ability to defile not only the person harboring the poison of bitterness but those under his sphere of influence.

That person who refuses to forgive has chosen the path of self-destruction and defilement in more ways than he realizes:

1. *Refusal to forgive turns one into a loser.* Someone has correctly said that the poison of an unforgiving spirit does more damage to the vessel in which it is stored than it does to the vessel on which it is poured. It turns him into a loser because he has chained himself to the person he refuses to forgive and has become his prisoner. Refusal to obey the Father and forgive is to pick a fight with Him that one cannot possibly win. This irrational choice turns the bitter, unforgiving person into a sore loser.

2. *Refusal to forgive makes enduring personal relationships impossible.* Personal relationships cannot survive apart from forgiveness. Friendships cannot survive unless friends learn to forgive friends. Marriages cannot survive without both mates learning the critical lesson of forgiving each other. Business relationships and partnerships inevitably fall apart without the essential element of forgiveness. The major life lesson of learning to forgive is one of the lessons of life that promotes emotional stability resulting in enduring personal relationships.

3. *Refusal to forgive engenders mental, emotional, physical, social, and spiritual problems.* A British doctor in charge of a large medical facility once stated that if all his patients could learn to forgive, a good number of them would be healed and could go home. One study from the *Journal of Behavioral Medicine* found forgiveness to lower the heart rate and blood pressure as well as stress. Forgiveness brings long-term health benefits.

The heart, mind, and soul cleansed by forgiveness will require fewer medications, have improved sleep quality, have reduced likelihood of depression, and suffer less fatigue. The reduction in the negative effects brought on by a bitter and unforgiving spirit strengthens one's spiritual walk with God and will have a significant impact on overall health.

Forgiveness restores positive thoughts and feelings toward the offending party that makes the restoration of broken relationships possible. Forgiveness also spills over to positive behaviors toward others outside of the broken relationship. Forgiveness is also associated with more volunteerism, donating to charity, and other altruistic behaviors.

4. *Refusal to forgive turns one into a bitter person.* An unforgiving spirit ferments bitterness, and bitterness turns the person who harbors its venom into its victim. It spreads like cancer throughout his entire being contaminating everything it touches. An unforgiving spirit will eventually turn a sweet person into a sour person, a pleasant person into an unpleasant person, and a happy person into a sad person. It will alter one's entire outlook on life, changing him into a negative person. An unforgiving spirit will turn on those who harbor it and destroy them.

5. *Refusal to forgive creates a bitter spirit that is contagious contaminating one's most loved and closest relatives and friends.* "Unforgiveness" is a deadly infectious spiritual disease. A bitter spirit is contagious, and tragically it infects those closest to the bitter person. Unforgiving bitter parents infect their children. Children of bitter parents have a skewed negative outlook on life and others. Friends of a bitter person will

either become bitter themselves or break the relationship for their good.

Bitterness cannot be compartmentalized. It spreads throughout a person's entire being. It poisons and contaminates his family and friends. It destroys any possibility of an intimate walk with God. It will eventually alter one's worldview from positive to negative. It will also create a negative view of all people instead of the original offending party. An unforgiving spirit is extremely dangerous to one's spiritual, social, and physical well-being.

Implications of an Unforgiving Heart

The person who professes to be a follower of Christ and refuses to forgive others raises serious questions about his relationship with Jesus.

It suggests that one has never experienced divine forgiveness. When one is saved and indwelt by the Holy Spirit, He floods the believer's heart with a supernatural love that automatically reaches out in forgiveness. An unforgiving spirit is so completely out of step with Bible Christianity that it legitimately raises the question of the authenticity of the reality of one's conversion.

It reveals that one is out of fellowship with God. It is impossible to be wrong with man and be right with God. The choice to refuse to forgive breaks fellowship with both God and the unforgiven offender.

It reveals a proud, self-centered heart that exalts self above Christ and His cause. The choice to forgive grows out of a humble heart. The choice not to forgive grows out of a proud me-centered heart that exalts self above Christ and His cause.

It reveals that one's spiritual growth has been stunted by a bitter, unforgiving spirit. Crisis experiences are providential growth opportunities. Spiritual giants grow by forgiving, while spiritual pygmies stunt their spiritual growth by refusing to forgive. Forgiveness is a spiritual fertilizer. Refusing to forgive is spiritual poison.

Christian Forgiveness Is Not Conditioned by an Apology

Jesus did not wait for an apology when He cried from the cross, "Father, forgive them for they do not know what they are doing." The offending party can go to their grave with a heart filled with bitterness and never offer the offended Christian an apology, but it remains incumbent upon the Christian to forgive them.

Christians forgive those who sin against them for several reasons. They forgive because their Lord commands them to forgive. They forgive because Christian forgiveness creates a positive witness to the world. Christians forgive others because forgiveness is the cleansing agent that purges their hearts from bitterness. Christian forgiveness is an opportunity for Christian growth that produces more mature Christians. Few things make a believer more Christlike than when he is forgiving others.

Christians are to be quick with a sincere apology. Although apologies reflect an earnest attempt at reconciliation, they are also very risky. An apology risks being viewed as the instigator of unpleasantness. An apology risks being ridiculed and perceived as being weak. An apology risks rejection and humiliation if the offended party rejects the apology and refuses to forgive. To give an earnest apology and to accept an apology both require a work of divine grace in the proud hearts of fallen men.

Refusing to forgive is out of character for a follower of Jesus Christ Who was all about forgiveness. The world's prime example of Christian forgiveness is His cry from the cross as He looked down on the milling mob that included those who had brutally beaten Him, nailed Him to the cross, and were mocking Him as He cried out, *Father, forgive them*. Forgiveness gives Christianity credibility. Forgiveness is a living illustration of Christlike character.

Life Lessons

"FORGIVE US OUR DEBTS, AS WE FORGIVE OUR DEBTORS"

Forgiveness is free to man, but it cost heaven its Crown Jewel.

Forgiveness does not imply God's acceptance or approval of sin.

Forgiveness does not negate all the consequences of sin.

The forgiven forgive.

Few things make one more Christlike than forgiveness

The bitterness of an unforgiving heart is caustic and contagious.

GOD'S PLAN FOR
VICTORIOUS CHRISTIAN LIVING

The Victor's Crown

GUIDE NO. 7

*Praying and Living by My Father's Plan on
How to Overcome Temptation*

Chapter 7

The Protection of the Father

And lead us not into temptation,
but deliver us from evil.
—*Matthew 6:13*

And cause us not to be led into temptation,
but rescue us from evil or the evil one.
—*Literal translation*

Introduction

God did not intend for His children to live defeated Christian lives. The fact that Jesus instructs believers in Matthew 6:13 to pray for divine guidance and deliverance means divine guidance and deliverance are available to those who pray and ask. As a loving heavenly Father, God will honor His previous guide and forgive those who pray and ask. This same loving Father will also honor His final guide and rescue from temptation those who pray and ask. As their loving Father, He has made provisions for His children to live victorious Christian lives.

The fact that divine deliverance from temptation is available brings up the question of why so many believers habitually succumb to temptation. The carnality of the modern church suggests that far too many believers are not taking advantage of Jesus's offer of deliverance from evil. Although there are other reasons, there are at least three primary reasons so many of God's children succumb to temptation.

First, they do not realize the evil nature of their *ruthless enemy*.

Second, many Christians do not realize how vulnerable their *ruined nature* makes them to temptation and how desperately they need God's help.

Third, many believers are not aware that God has a *real plan* on how to overcome temptation and how His plan works.

A Ruthless Enemy

Jesus instructs believers to earnestly pray for divine guidance and deliverance from evil or the evil one. He gives these instructions because they are facing a powerful and ruthless enemy and desperately need help. Before believers ever seek God's directions and deliverance, they must first be made aware that they are engaged in a life and death struggle with a ruthless enemy who is devoid of character. The Word of God compares him to a roaring lion seeking to devour his prey. God warns believers, "Beware, be vigilant; because your adversary the devil walks about like a roaring lion, seeking whom he may devour" (1 Pet. 5:8).

Jesus describes him as follows, "He was a murderer from the beginning, and does not stand in the truth, because there is no truth in him. When he speaks a lie, he speaks from his own resources, for he is a liar, and the father of it" (John 8:44). Jesus defines the believer's ruthless enemy as a liar and the father of lies. Being the father of lies means that his primary tactic in tempting believers to sin is deception. Jesus further defines the believers' ruthless enemy as a murderer from the beginning which means that he places no value on human life. The devil's thrill is to kill.

The three primary tactics of this ruthless enemy are deception, defilement, and destruction. As the master of deception, the devil seeks to deceive sinners into viewing themselves as superior to God. Next, he seeks to convince them that sin is good and God is bad. His goal is to defile God's most treasured creation by contaminating them with sin. Finally, his ultimate goal is to destroy them by any means possible. This ruthless enemy has no regard for the pain and suffering he inflicts on mankind. He is completely devoid of love or compassion.

As the believer's ruthless supernatural enemy, the devil must be engaged on a spiritual level with the Father's supernatural assistance. A rough paraphrase of 2 Corinthians 10:3–4 says the following about engaging this cruel enemy: "Although we do live in a body of flesh, we do not engage this enemy in our flesh. For the weapons of our warfare are not carnal but mighty through God for the pulling down of the enemy's fortresses." No believer is ever able to engage this ruthless enemy in his flesh. He will lose every time. He must always rely on divine assistance.

The Apostle Paul describes the nature of this battle as follows, "For we do not wrestle against flesh and blood, but against principalities (rulers), against powers, against rulers of the darkness of this age, against spiritual wickedness in heavenly places" (Eph. 6:12). The enemy is not human; he is not flesh and blood. He is far more powerful than any human. He is the ruler of the fallen world of darkness and demons. His domain is darkened by evil. The Devil is a real and a ruthless enemy.

A Ruined Nature

Concerning the ruined nature of his flesh and its natural inclinations toward sin, Paul wrote, "For I know that in me (that is, in my body) nothing good dwells; for to will is present with me, but how to perform what is good I do not find" (Rom. 7:18). He would later cry out, "O wretched man that I am! Who will deliver me from this body of death?" Then in a great shout of victory, he cried out, "I thank God— through JESUS CHRIST OUR LORD!" (Rom. 7:24–25). Jesus has provided a plan for victory over the flesh and over Satan that will be elaborated below. However, before delving into Jesus's sure plan for victorious Christian living, it will help to have a better understanding of the depths of the believer's depraved nature that he must also do battle with.

First, the flesh (carnal nature) of the redeemed is still unredeemed. The flesh of a saved person is just as depraved after salvation as it was before conversion. Paul writes that Christians await the future redemption of their bodies (Rom. 8:23). Therefore, the believer must keep a constant guard upon his unredeemed flesh. Only by reliance upon the indwelling Holy Spirit, the Word, and prayer can the believer control his unregenerate flesh. This unregenerate flesh means that the greatest saints are still capable of the greatest sins. Never trust the flesh!

Second, the flesh can never be satisfied. The temptation to give into the flesh is a solicitation to yield to an insatiable appetite. To yield to sin only creates a greater appetite and capacity for sin. The fallen, sinful nature of man is never satisfied. It will always demand more. The rich desire more riches. The powerful desire more power. Immorality creates a greater desire and capacity for immorality. Normal sexual promiscuity can evolve into sexual perversion of the vilest kind. The flesh will always demand something a little more alluring and exciting. The more one gives into his flesh, the more it will demand. Never trust the flesh!

Third, the flesh never counts the cost. The flesh never reminds the individual that its demands could cost him his wife, his family, his friends, his career, and even his life. Anyone who has been in church long has heard the saying that "sin will take you farther than you ever intended to go, keep you longer than you ever intended to stay, and cost you more than you ever intended to pay." The wrecked and ruined lives scattered along life's highway serve as undeniable proof that the flesh never counts the cost of gratifying its selfish, sinful desires. Never trust the flesh!

Fourth, the flesh is self-centered. The flesh cares only for itself and self-gratification. The flesh will never remind the individual that what he is about to do will cause great hurt and harm to himself, his mate, family, friends, career, or whatever. The fallen flesh is so self-centered that it will risk or even sacrifice the lives and love of others to gratify itself. It will jeopardize everything precious to an individual to gratify itself. Never trust the flesh!

Fifth, the flesh has no conscience. Once the flesh is aroused, it has little or no concern over morality. Once the passions of the flesh are stirred, the flesh uses irrational logic to justify its contemplated evil desires. The flesh can, by irrational justification of its contemplated evil actions, blind or sear the conscience. Once an individual's passions are stirred, he will justify his sinful desires and actions. Never trust the flesh!

Sixth, with the flesh, it is rule or ruin. Either a child of God, by the enabling power of the Holy Spirit, the living Word of God, and prayer, rules his flesh or it will rule him. The flesh will enslave and ultimately destroy its victim. The flesh hates a disciplined life. Restraint is not a part of its vocabulary. The fallen nature of man resents all outside authority and desires complete control. Once it gains control of an individual, it will ultimately destroy him. Either he rules his flesh or it will rule and ultimately ruin him. Never trust the flesh!

Seventh, nobody can control or tame his flesh. Paul recognized his inability to control his flesh and cried out in desperation, "O wretched man that I am! Who will deliver me from this body of death?" Paul had come to the very end of himself and did not see his deliverance coming from within. In his next statement, he expressed with great gratitude that he had found the help needed to overcome his flesh and the world when he wrote, "I thank God—through Jesus Christ our Lord" (Rom. 7:24–25). Paul further expressed how to control the flesh when he wrote, "Walk in the Spirit and you will not fulfill the desires of the flesh" (Gal. 5:16). Jesus overcame temptation by quoting the Scriptures (Matt. 4:4, 7, 10).

The above truths about the believer's ruthless enemy and his ruined nature are designed to bring every child of God to the very end of any reliance upon himself and his flesh to overcome temptation. Only then will he follow God's real plan and turn to God in instant prayer when faced by the evil solicitations of his ruthless enemy as he moves to deceive, defile, and destroy him.

A Real Plan

God has in place a real plan on how to overcome temptation. Because this plan originated in the mind of an omniscient and omnipotent God, it works every time it is applied. Believers can live a victorious Christian life! The fact that so many believers live defeated lives is not a reflection on God's perfect plan. It is a reflection on their failure to follow God's plan.

The fallen nature of the believer naturally looks for three or four simple, easy steps on how to overcome temptation and live the victorious Christian life. What would be even better than three easy steps would be a spiritual pill one could take every morning that would guarantee an overcoming victorious Christian life. The good news is that God does have a real plan that comes with His divine warranty that it will work every time it is applied.

God's Comprehensive Plan

God has not left His children defenseless before their ruthless enemy and their depraved nature. His authoritative Word declares that He has a comprehensive plan that will guarantee victory over every temptation any of His children will ever face. It has been tried and tested under the fire by the believer's High Priest Who "was in all points tempted as we are, yet without *sin*" (Heb. 4:15). This plan is instantly activated by coming boldly to the throne of grace in time of need (Heb. 4:14-16). In the following passage, Paul gives believers four great truths about God's real plan that assures them of victory:

> No temptation has overtaken you except such as is common to man; but God is faithful, who will not allow you to be tempted beyond what you are able, but with the temptation will also make *the way of escape*, that you may be able to bear it. (1 Cor. 10:13)

God pledges to every believer under the stress of temptation that He already has in place not "a" *way of escape*, but "*the*" *way of escape* from any temptation they will ever face. This text does not give the details of God's plan on how to overcome temptation. It gives four great assurances of the comprehensive nature of God's plan. It is God's divine guarantee that they can overcome any temptation they will ever face.

First, they can overcome every temptation because the temptation they face is not unique. They are not the first believers to ever face this temptation; it is *common to man*. Others have faced and overcome this same temptation. Therefore, they can also overcome.

Second, they can overcome every temptation because *God is faithful*. He will always be there with them in times of temptation. No child of God ever faces temptation alone. The Father never abandons any of His children in their time of need.

Third, they can overcome every temptation because their faithful God *will not allow you to be tempted beyond what you are able*. He knows the limitations of each of His children and will never allow the devil to overwhelm them. God's grace is always available, and it is always sufficient.

Fourth, they can overcome every temptation because their Father has provided "the" *way of escape* from any temptation they will ever face. The definite article "the" before the noun "way" means that God already has in place the specific plan of escape designed specifically for every temptation any of His children will ever face.

The author of Hebrews also offers some strong encouragement to believers who are facing temptation. He reminds them that their faithful High Priest has walked in their shoes. He was tempted in all points like them and can empathize with them. He also extends a gracious offer to help those who ask:

> For we do not have a High Priest, who cannot sympathize with our weaknesses but was in all points

tempted as we are, yet without sin. Let us, therefore, come boldly to the throne of grace, that we
may obtain mercy and find grace to help in time of
need. (Heb. 4:15–16)

This passage relates four great truths to comfort and empower believers
when they are tempted.

First, believers have a *sympathetic* High Priest Who can relate to them
when they are tempted because He was also tempted in all points like
them.

Second, believers have a *victorious* High Priest Who was tempted like
them and overcame every temptation and remained sinless.

Third, believers have a *gracious* High Priest Who offers mercy and grace
to those who come boldly to the throne and ask.

Finally, believers have a *powerful* High Priest Who stands patiently
waiting to extend mercy and grace and deliver those who come boldly
to Him in their time of temptation.

A Victorious Plan

Because Jesus is the believer's ideal example, His plan for victory over
the temptations of the devil in the wilderness becomes their plan for
victory. It is interesting how the tactics Jesus employed in that situa-
tion harmonize so well with what the New Testament teaches in other
passages on how to overcome temptation. Given below is an analysis of
the tactics Jesus employed in His victory over Satan in the wilderness.

It is given along with a comparison of what other New Testament passages say on the tactics on overcoming temptation[8]:

> Then Jesus was *led up by the Spirit* into the wilderness to be tempted by the devil. And when He had *fasted* (and prayed) *forty days and forty nights*, afterward He was hungry. Now when the tempter came to Him, he said, "If You are the Son of God, command that these stones become bread." But He answered and said, "*It is written*, 'Man shall not live by bread alone, but by every word that proceeds from the mouth of God.'" Then the devil took Him up into the holy city, set Him on the pinnacle of the temple, and said to Him, "If You are the Son of God, throw Yourself down. For it is written: 'He shall give His angels charge over you,' and, 'In their hands they shall bear you up, Lest you dash your foot against a stone.'" Jesus said to him, "*It is written again*, 'You shall not tempt the Lord your God.'" Again, the devil took Him up on an exceedingly high mountain, and showed Him all the kingdoms of the world and their glory. And he said to Him, "All these things I will give You if You will fall down and worship me." Then Jesus said to him, "Away with you, Satan! *For it is written*, 'You shall worship the Lord your God, and Him only you shall serve.'" Then the devil left

---

[8] The five traits of an overcomer are given with the supporting verses: (1) watchfulness (Matt. 26:41, Eph. 6:18), (2) faith (Heb. 4:16, Eph. 6:16), (3) Holy Spirit (Rom. 8:2–4, Gal. 5:16, Eph. 6:18), (4) Word (Matt. 4:4, 7, 10; Eph. 6:17), and (5) prayer (Matt. 4:2, 26:41; Heb. 4:16; Eph. 6:18).

Him, and behold, angels came and ministered to
Him. (Matt. 4:1–11)

First, Jesus overcame temptation by being *a man of faith*. Jesus prayed
and fasted because He had faith that His Father would hear and answer
His prayers. He quoted the Scriptures when tempted because He had
faith in the power of the living Word of the living God. The incarnate
Son of God instructed His disciples to pray for deliverance from temptation because He had faith that God had a plan for deliverance.

Paul's view on the importance of faith is reflected in his words "above
all" in his inclusion of the shield of faith as a vital part of the whole
armor of God in Ephesians 6:10–20. In verse 16, he wrote, "Above
all, taking the shield of faith with which you will be able to quench all
the fiery darts of the wicked one." Faith renders the attractions of the
temptations of the wicked one powerless by casting the tempted upon
prayer, the Word, and the Holy Spirit for victory.

None of the other tools given for overcoming temptation work apart
from faith. Until a believer believes that he can trust God to deliver
him from the temptations of the evil one, he is never going to pray for
deliverance. Until he believes that the Word of God is alive and powerful, he is never going to rely on it when facing temptation. Until he
believes that the Holy Spirit can and will empower and enable him to
overcome temptation, he will seek in vain to overcome temptation in
his flesh and fail. Faith activates prayer, the Word, and the Holy Spirit
in overcoming temptation.

Second, Jesus overcame temptation by being *a watchful person (verse 2)*.
Jesus spent forty days in prayer and fasting before being tempted by
Satan. These were precautionary actions to prepare and arm Himself
against the coming temptations. James admonishes believers to first

"submit to God and then resist the devil, and he will flee from you" (James 4:7). Paul urged believers to be "praying always with all prayer and supplication in the Spirit, *being watchful* to this end with all perseverance and supplication for all the saints" (Eph. 6:18). Peter warns, "Be sober, be vigilant; because your adversary the devil walks about like a roaring lion, seeking whom he may devour" (1 Pet. 5:8). Jesus warned His disciples to "*Watch* and pray, lest you enter into temptation. The spirit indeed is willing, but the flesh is weak" (Matt. 26:41). The devious schemes of a ruthless enemy and the natural inclinations of the flesh toward sin both demand a constant vigil on the part of the overcomer.

Third, Jesus overcame temptation *by relying upon the Holy Spirit (verse 1).* The Word of God says, "Then Jesus was led by the Spirit into the wilderness to be tempted by the devil." This harmonizes perfectly with what the Word teaches when Paul advises believers to "walk in the Spirit, and you will not fulfill the works of the flesh" (Gal. 5:16). The defeated Christian of Romans 7 becomes the victorious Christian of Romans 8 by the power of the indwelling Holy Spirit Who is cited sixteen times in chapter 8. Verses 2–4 speak directly to the enabling power of the Holy Spirit in overcoming temptation and sin:

> For the law of the Spirit of life in Christ Jesus has made me free from the law of sin and death. [3]For what the law could not do in that it was weak through the flesh, God *did* by sending His own Son in the likeness of sinful flesh, on account of sin: He condemned sin in the flesh, *that the righteous requirement of the law might be fulfilled in us who do not walk according to the flesh but according to the Spirit.* (Rom. 8:2–4).

Victorious Christians overcome temptation when they come to the very end of any reliance upon themselves and their flesh to resist and overcome temptation. The proud heart must be humbled and broken before God. Self must be dethroned and Jesus enthroned. The Lord will then fill and anoint with His Holy Spirit as the Divine Enabler to overcome temptation.

Fourth, Jesus overcame temptation *by relying upon the Word of God.* On each occasion the devil tempted Him, Jesus responded by quoting the powerful and living Word of God (Matt. 4:4, 7, 10). Jesus's use of the Word in confronting temptation testifies to His confidence in the supernatural power of God's Word. In His high priestly prayer for His disciples and subsequent believers in John 17:17, Jesus prays to the Father, "Sanctify them by Your truth. Your Word is truth."

Paul made reliance upon the Word a vital part of the whole armor of God necessary to withstand the devious tactics of the devil. He wrote, "And take the helmet of salvation, and the sword of the Spirit, which is the word of God" (Eph. 6:17). He equated the Word of God to a powerful offensive and defensive weapon when he referred to it as the "sword of the spirit." The living and powerful Word of God describes itself as follows, "For the word of God is living and powerful, and sharper than any two-edged sword, piercing even to the division of soul and spirit, and of joints and marrow, and is a discerner of the thoughts and intents of the heart" (Heb. 4:12).

Fifth, Jesus overcame temptation *by praying and fasting.* The text says, "And when He had fasted forty days and forty nights, afterward He was hungry" (verse 2). In the Scriptures, prayer and fasting always go together. Jesus instructed His disciples in the garden to watch "and *pray* lest you enter into temptation, for the spirit is willing, but the flesh is weak" (Matt. 26:41). He instructed His disciples in Matthew 6:13 to pray, "Lead us not into temptation but deliver us from evil." Prayer is a vital part of the "whole armor of God" necessary to defeat the devil. Paul instructed believers to be "praying always with all prayer and supplication in the Spirit, being watchful to this end with all perseverance and supplication for all the saints" (Eph. 6:18).

A Simple Plan

Jesus's final guide on deliverance from evil and the evil one does not mention watchfulness, faith, the Word, or the Holy Spirit which He used in overcoming the temptation in the wilderness. Instead, Jesus instructs believers to do one thing. When faced with temptation, they are to pray the simple prayer, *Lead us not into temptation but deliver us from evil.* This same concept of immediately turning to God in prayer in time of need is also stated by the author of Hebrews when he writes, "Let us therefore come boldly to the throne of grace, that we may obtain mercy and find grace to help in time of need." (Heb. 4:16).

The nature of prayer makes it the believer's most potent offensive and defensive weapon. Jesus's final guide reveals that a believer's immediate reaction when faced with temptation determines his victory or defeat. Jesus is warning believers never to take time to deliberate when faced with temptation. Never give the flesh the opportunity to justify yielding to temptation and gratifying its selfish carnal desires. Prayer must be the believer's instant response when tempted.

"Lead us not into temptation, but deliver us from evil," is a spiritual SOS to God's divine rescue squad for deliverance. It only arises from a desperate heart that has come to the end of any reliance upon the flesh to overcome temptation. This urgent prayer of faith summons into action a supernatural rescue and deliverance team composed of the Father, the Son, the Holy Spirit, and the living Word. They are an invincible team instantly available to deliver any believer who, in faith, turns to them in urgent and earnest prayer to rescue them from temptation.

When Jesus instructed believers to pray, "Lead us not into temptation, but deliver us from evil." He was making the following promise. Those who earnestly pray this simple prayer in faith can instantly summons the Father, the Son, the Holy Spirit, and the Word into action to rescue them from temptation.

God's plan for deliverance from temptation works every time it is applied. It can be summed up into two simple steps of faith.

1. The first step in overcoming temptation is overcoming any temptation to trust in self.
2. The second step in overcoming temptation is instant earnest prayer for God's deliverance.

Life Lessons

"LEAD US NOT INTO TEMPTATION BUT DELIVER US FROM EVIL"

God has a plan for victory over every temptation.

God's plan for victory over temptation works every time it is applied.

God's plan for victory over temptation is activated by prayer.

God's plan for victory over temptation casts one upon the Holy Spirit, prayer, and His Word.

God's plan for victory only works for the desperate who have come to the end of themselves.

MAJESTIC IN GLORY
GLORIOUS IN MAJESTY

Prayer should conclude with a focus on God
Prayer should conclude on a positive note of praise
Prayers addressed to the King of an everlasting Kingdom live forever.
Prayers addressed to an all-powerful King are invincible.

Chapter 8

The Praise of the Father

For Yours is the kingdom, the power,
and the glory forever. Amen.
—Matthew 6:13

Introduction

This doxology is not in any manuscripts of Luke. It is also missing in the oldest manuscripts of Matthew. Most modern critical texts and translations do not include this closing doxology because most textual scholars do not view it as a part of the original autographs. That discussion will be left to those more competent in textual matters. It is included as a part of this study because, regardless of whether it was included in the original text, the concepts developed are thoroughly biblical. It is almost universally accepted as the conclusion of the Lord's Prayer, and it concludes prayer on a positive note with a shout of victory and praise.

A Declaration of the Father's Uniqueness

This doxology is a declaration that the Father has an invincible, powerful, and glorious kingdom that will never end. In the original language, all three nouns, *kingdom, power,* and *glory,* are preceded by the definite article "the." In the Greek language, the definite article serves to identify and set them apart from all other kingdoms, powers, and glories. They are not "a" kingdom, "a" power, and "a" glory. They are "the" kingdom, "the" power, and "the" glory. They are in an exclusive class all by themselves. No other kingdom, power, or glory can compare with them. They are unique because the Father is unique, and they are an extension of Who He is.

The hope of the Father's children is not dependent upon the political machinations of mortal man and the rise and fall of passing kings and kingdoms. Their hope is in their Father and His unique kingdom which is invincible and eternal because He is invincible and eternal. His kingdom is the most glorious kingdom ever to exist because He is the most glorious king ever to exist. His glory will illuminate the new earth and its capital city, the New Jerusalem. When a believer closes his prayer with the concept *For yours is the kingdom and the power and the glory forever. Amen,* he is concluding his conversation with his Father with a strong positive declaration of his faith in His unique "one of a kind" heavenly Father and His glorious eternal kingdom.

A Declaration of the Father's Sovereign Power

The clause *For Yours is the kingdom* could be translated *Because You are the kingdom.* It suggests that He is the *source* and *cause* of its origin, and that is why it is *His* kingdom. The possessive pronoun *Yours* is also an affirmation of His *ownership* of the kingdom, the power, and the glory. He is the originator, owner, and operator of "the" kingdom, "the" power, and "the" glory.[9]

---

[9] Creation was a joint project of the Trinity, but Jesus was the active agent in creation. This explains why John wrote of Jesus, "He made all things; and without Him was not anything made that was made... He was in the world, and he made

The thing that guarantees His sovereign rule and authority over His kingdom is the fact that He is the originating source of all the power and energy in existence. All power and energy in existence are delegated from God. As the originator and owner, He controls all power. Nothing or nobody moves unless He approves by delegating them the energy or power to move. His is "the" power source that energizes His kingdom.

Kings rule only by His permission and at His discretion. Being the originating source of all power, kings only possess the limited power He sovereignly grants them. Their rule and authority are always temporary, while His are designated as being "forever." An illustration of the Father's infinite power that guarantees His sovereignty is seen that He once dispatched one angel who slew 185,000 soldiers in one night.

David was right on target when he proclaimed, "Yours, O LORD, is the greatness and the power and the glory and the victory and the majesty, indeed everything that is in the heavens and the earth; Yours is the dominion, O LORD, and You exalt Yourself as head over all" (1 Chron. 29:11).

A Declaration of the Father's Infinite Glory

The Father's glory is not "a" glory among many glories. It is "the" glory that distinguishes it from all other glories in existence. It is this unique glory that eliminates any need for the sun, moon, and stars in the New

---

the world, and the world knew Him not. But as many as received Him, to them He gave the power to become the sons of God, even to them that believe on His name" (John 1:3, 10, 12). Paul also recognized Jesus as the active member in creation when he wrote, "For by Him were all things created, that are in heaven, and that are in earth, visible and invisible, whether they be thrones, or dominions, or principalities, or powers: all things were created by Him, and for Him: And He is before all things, and by Him all things consist [are held together]" (Col. 1:16–17).

Jerusalem, which is heaven's capital city. The text says, "And the city had no need of the sun or the moon to shine in it, for the glory of God illuminated it, and the Lamb is its light" (Rev. 21:23).

The author of this doxology, *Yours is the kingdom, the power, and the glory, forever*, was following the lead of the saints of all the ages in their worship and praise of their God for His dominion, His power, and His glory. The book of Revelation is laden with doxologies of praise. The following passage depicts a future universal scene of praise to God for His dominion, His power, and His glory:

> Then I looked, and I heard the voice of many angels around the throne, the living creatures, and the elders; and the number of them was ten thousand times ten thousand, and thousands of thousands, saying with a loud voice: "Worthy is the Lamb who was slain to receive power and riches and wisdom, And strength and honor and glory and blessing!" And I heard every creature which is in heaven and on the earth and under the earth and such as are in the sea, and all that are in them, I heard saying: *Blessing and honor and glory and power Be to Him who sits on the throne, And to the Lamb, forever and* [a]*ever!* (Rev. 5:11–13)

As cited above, David offers this same type of praise in one of the most definitive doxologies in the Scriptures. This extraordinary doxology of praise demands being given in its entirety:

> Yours, O Lord, is the greatness, The power and the glory, The victory and the majesty; For all that is in heaven and in earth is Yours; Yours is the kingdom,

O LORD, And You are exalted as head over all. Both riches and honor come from You, And You reign over all. In Your hand is power and might; In Your hand it is to make great And to give strength to all.

Now, therefore, our God, We thank You And praise Your glorious name. (1 Chron. 29:11–13)

Every step that believers take in heaven will be in the manifest presence of the glory of God that illuminates the new earth and the New Jerusalem. His dazzlingly, brilliant, radiant glory that emanates from His glorious person will bring with it a continuous reminder of His glorious presence with His children forever. Every nook and cranny in all of creation will be illuminated by God's dazzling glory except the darkness of hell that the Bible refers to as "outer darkness" (Matt. 8:12). This concluding doxology speaks to the indescribable majesty of the Father's glory.

A Declaration of the Durability of the Father's Kingdom, Power, and Glory *Forever*

The Greeks had an interesting way of saying "forever" or "everlasting." They would say "unto the ages." When they used this phrase, they meant that if the ages are continuously piled upon the ages, the King, and His kingdom, His power, and His glory, would still be standing. Unlike earthly kings and kingdoms, which are all temporary and passing, this King and His kingdom, power, and glory will endure for ages piled upon ages to the extent that they never expire.

Because humans live in a world of beginnings and endings, it is extremely difficult for the human mind to grasp the concept of God as being without beginning and ending. Everything about them has a beginning; it then ages, decays, and dies. Because of the curse, all humans know that the aging process brings in its wake decay and death. The concept of moving into a majestic kingdom untouched by the curse of sin (Rev. 22:3) where there is no aging that brings decay and death is a mind-boggling concept affirmed in this doxology.

The viability of this "forever" concept grows out the fact that the King inhabits eternity and lives above time. He created time as a tool to measure the aging and decaying process brought on by the fall and the curse of sin. Also, because God is perfectly holy and therefore untouched by the curse of sin, He is unaffected by time. God is no older today than when He created time. He is the same today, yesterday, and forever (Heb. 13:8). God, Who inhabits eternity, never ages (Isa. 57:15).

The King of this "forever" kingdom never had a beginning and will never have an ending (Heb. 7:3; Rev. 22:13). The eternality of the King is the guarantee of the eternality of His kingdom. Only an eternal King can grant eternal life to His subjects that guarantees that they will never die (John 10:28). This is a forever King with a forever kingdom inhabited by forever citizens. Amen!

Conclusion

Summarize, Simplify, Apply

Jesus never taught just to share information. He always taught to change lives. Jesus expects His followers to think, pray, and live guided by His seven powerful and transformative guides contained in the Lord's Prayer. He gave these guides primarily as prayer guides. However, if Jesus expects His followers to pray to God as their Father, He obviously expects them to live like God is their Father. If He expects them to pray subject to their Father's will, He also expects them to live subject to His will. This principle applies to each of Jesus's seven guides which makes them both prayer and life guides.

There is nothing wrong with quoting, praying, or singing the Lord's Prayer since it is a part of the inspired, inerrant, and authoritative, living Word of the living God. However, the Lord's Prayer will impact one's life spiritually only to the degree that its message is understood and applied. The preceding chapters were devoted to an in-depth analysis of meaning and implications of Jesus's guides on prayer because prayer and life are inseparable. The transformative power of prayer molds and shapes the lives of those who pray. Nobody is ever any more powerful than he is prayerful. No believer ever rises above his prayer life.

This conclusion is designed to summarize, simplify, and apply Jesus's prayer and life guides to life. Properly understood and applied, they will transform God's children into powerful prayer warriors and effective witnesses whose lives will impact their culture with the gospel of Jesus Christ.

Guide No. 1

Summarize

Our Father: Christians are to perceive of, relate to, and pray to God as their heavenly Father. This can only happen by being born into His family by the new birth. Once this happens, they are to perceive of themselves as the elect children of God chosen in Christ before the creation of the world (Eph. 1:4). This transaction restores their original and authentic identity as unique children of God fully loved and accepted by their Father. Their heavenly Father has endowed them with gifts and talents which, when mixed with their unique personalities, set them apart as unique and special children of God with a role in His kingdom which no one on earth can fulfill like them. This identity as the children of God provides them with a genuine purpose in life as well as a sense of self-worth that makes life meaningful. God's children know who they are, how they got here, why they are here, and where they are going. As their Father's unique children, He will hear and answer their prayers.

Simplify

> *Christians have been born into their Father's family by the new birth which identifies them as His unique children who are fully loved and accepted in Christ whose prayers He hears and answers.*

Guide No. 2

Summarize

Hallowed be Your name: In His second guide, Jesus requires those who pray effectively to recognize God's requirement for them to reverence and awe their heavenly Father as being above all things holy (Exod. 15:11; Lev. 11:44–45, 19:2, 20:7; 1 Pet. 1:15–16; Isa. 1:4, 6:3, 40:25, 57:15; Rev. 4:8). Any concept of God that does not recognize holiness as His number 1 moral attribute is not the biblical concept of the holy God revealed in the Christian Scriptures. Unbelievers live for their glory. The Father's children live for the glory of their Father (1 Cor. 10:31). The cause that captivates and drives them is His glory, and He cannot be glorified apart from hallowing His name as holy. Unholy people cannot hallow the name of a holy God as holy. Effectual prayer can only emanate from a believer who reverences his Father's name as holy and lives a holy life.

Simplify

> *Christians pray and live to reverence and glorify their Father's name as holy as the primary purpose of their lives.*

Guide No. 3

Summarize

Your kingdom come: This third guide refers to the "coming" of a spiritual kingdom which is already present that can only be accessed by being born into it by repenting and believing (Mark 1:15; John 3:3, 5). It also refers to a coming literal millennial kingdom on this present sin-cursed earth (Rev. 20:1–10) and a literal kingdom paradise on the new earth (Rev. 21–22). This kingdom only "comes" through evangelism since it can only be accessed by being born into it by the new birth (John 3:3, 5; 2 Pet. 1:10–11). Jesus came to seek and save the lost through evangelism (Luke 19:10). His Great Commission to His church is a charge to evangelize the nations (Mark 16:15; Matt. 28:18–20). Believers are to pray and live as pilgrim witnesses who do not sink their roots too deeply in this passing world as they are engaged in evangelism to advance the coming of the kingdom rule and authority of their King in the hearts of men.

Simplify

> *Christians are kingdom Christians born into the kingdom by the new birth who pray and live in anticipation of the coming of their King and His literal kingdom while they are busy advancing the coming of His kingdom rule and authority in the hearts of the unsaved through evangelism.*

Guide No. 4

Summarize

Your will be done: This fourth guide is the center guide because none of the others work apart from submission to the Father's will. Nobody can gain access into the kingdom apart from submission to the King of the kingdom (Matt. 7:21). God's will, which is primarily revealed in His Word, is how He requires men to think, pray, and live based on Who He is in the deepest recesses of His holy and loving being. Because He is holy (perfectly pure) and loving, God's will always functions for His glory and men's highest good. God's will is knowable (Eph. 5:17) and doable (Matt. 6:10; Prov. 3:5–6). The center of His will is the safest, most rewarding, most fulfilling, and happiest place a believer can be (Heb. 10:36).

Simplify

> *The highest authority in a Christian's life is the holy and loving will of his Father which is revealed primarily in His Word and always functions for His glory and the believer's highest good.*

Guide No. 5

Summarize

Give us this day our daily bread: This fifth guide requires Christians to pray and live totally dependent upon their Father for their entire existence both spiritually and physically. This guide constitutes a daily dose of *humility* because it is a daily reminder to believers that it is *in Him, we live and move and have our being* (Acts 17:28). This mandate to pray daily for one's daily bread is also a call from a loving Father for *daily fellowship* with His children. This daily prayer for bread and the Father's supply results in *increased faith* in the Father to meet one's needs which also reduces *undue stress and anxiety* about bread for tomorrow. It is a great day in the life of any believer when he learns to lean on his holy and loving Father as the most important resource of his life.

Simplify

> *Christians pray and live daily in total dependence upon their Father, not only for their daily bread but also for their entire existence.*

Guide No. 6

Summarize

Forgive us our debts as we forgive our debtors. Jesus' sixth guide is a declaration of a holy Father's hatred for sin and sinful men's desperate need of forgiveness and reconciliation. This guide is predicated on the facts that sin alienates believers from their Lord and they desperately need to be forgiven and restored to favor and fellowship with Him. This guide requires believers to follow their Lord's example and graciously forgive those who sin against them as a testimony to a perishing world of the reality of Christianity.

Simplify

> *Christians fear sin and value purity which requires*
> *their Father's daily forgiveness and cleansing while*
> *they gladly forgive those who sin against them.*

Guide No. 7

Summarize

Lead us not into temptation but deliver us from evil. The fact that Jesus instructs believers to pray for divine guidance when tempted and deliverance from evil dictates that God has in place a guaranteed plan on how to secure His guidance and deliverance. As a divine plan, it works every time it is applied. God never intended for sin to have dominion over His children. He has in place a plan on how His children can live victorious Christian lives.

This plan requires that a believer first come to the very end of himself and any reliance on his flesh to face the Devil and overcome his temptations. He must by faith instantly and prayerfully casts himself totally upon his heavenly Father, His Word, and the indwelling Holy Spirit when faced by temptation. Every temptation is faced and overcome by instant prayer because the prayer of faith includes all these essentials in overcoming temptation. God's plan always works. Believers can live a victorious Christian life.

Simplify

> *When faced with temptation, Christians immediately turn*
> *to their Father in prayer and cast themselves upon Him*
> *for His guidance and deliverance from temptation.*

Apply

Powerful Prayer

Prayer is powerful and transformative. Prayer does not change an immutable (changeless) God; it changes the person who prays. One of the most defining things about a person and their walk with God is their prayer life. How a person prays determines how he lives. The two are inseparable. People live like they pray. If they do not pray, they live like they do not pray. The transformative power of prayer determines the focus of a person's life.

Jesus gave these guides to transform believers into effective prayer warriors and powerful witnesses. It is good to sing and pray them as the Lord's Prayer, but unless one understands what he is singing or praying, their transforming power is very limited. He is basically performing a religious ritual. However, properly understood and applied, these guides become one of God's most powerful tools in transforming lives.

Proper Perspective

Jesus's seven guides also determine the proper focus of a believer's prayers and his life. Our Lord is very careful to begin by focusing prayer *upward* upon God, then *outward* upon others, and finally *inward* upon one's self. This is Jesus's balanced and biblical focus for the prayers and the lives of His Father's children. Any deviation from this divine order is devastating to the individual believer as well as the church. The finite wisdom of man can never improve on the infinite wisdom of God.

The natural inclination of the selfish carnal nature of fallen men is to reverse Jesus's divine order and shift the primary focus from God and others to self. This reversal of God's divine order will result in a gradual transition from worshipping the holy God of the Bible to worshipping a permissive carnal god of love. Inward focused Christianity will always devolve into a self-centered carnal Christianity. It is natural for the depraved flesh to seek to create for itself a carnal god of love who tolerates its carnal cravings and lifestyle.

Prescribed Practices

Jesus's seven guides do focus upon the priority of prayer and a biblical balance of the believer's prayers and life, but they also focus on the seven key practices of the Christian life given below:

- A Christian knows, relates to, prays to, and lives like God is his Father.
- A Christian prays and lives to glorify his Father's name as holy.

- A Christian prays and lives to advance the coming of his Father's kingdom primarily through personal evangelism.
- A Christian prays and lives subject to his Father's will.
- A Christian prays and lives in total dependence upon his Father for his entire existence.
- A Christian has a healthy fear of sin and its tragic consequences and prays for his Father's forgiveness and cleansing while forgiving others.
- A Christian does not trust his flesh and immediately casts himself in prayer upon his Father for His guidance and deliverance when tempted.

Primary Priorities

"Our Father" makes knowing God as one's Father the most important *relationship* of the Christian life.

"Hallowed be Your Name" makes glorifying God as holy the most important *reason* for the Christian life.

"Your Kingdom Come" makes the coming of God's Kingdom rule and authority in the hearts of the unsaved through evangelism the most important *role* of the Christian life.

"Your Will be Done" makes the will of God the most important *rule* of the Christian life.

"Give Us this Day our Daily Bread" makes God the most important *resource* of the Christian life.

"Forgive Us our Sins as We forgive those Who have sinned against Us" makes being forgiven and forgiving others the most important *reconciliations* of the Christian life.

"Lead Us not into Temptation but deliver Us from Evil" makes God's deliverance the most important *rescue* of the Christian life.

Only God could compact so much vital information into the approximately sixty-five words five verses. It is the earnest prayer of this author that Jesus will choose to use this analysis of His seven guides on how to pray and live to transform millions of His children into powerful prayer warriors and witnesses. When this happens, their lives and churches can be summarized by the following motto:

"To Know Him and Make Him Known from My House to the Regions Beyond"

The Final Victor

(A poetic response to the rise and fall of Humanism)

Mayberry USA has gone its way,
Humanism is now the rage of the day.
Sin is now good, and God is now bad,
Right is now wrong in a country gone mad.
Bible Christianity is viewed as a relic of the past,
An ancient pagan religion seeks to conquer America at last.
Humanism has moved America from grace to disgrace,
God's divine moral code is now out of place.
America now worships at the shrine of human reason,
God's Ten Commandments are now out of season.
Human reason governs America's new way,
The Bible is banned from having any say.
Rebellious man is having his final fling,
Deified human reason is America's new king.
Humanism's ungodly reign will soon fade away,
King Jesus's righteous reign will have full sway.
Humanists now enforce their ungodly plans,
But history is controlled by God's sovereign hands.
When the last shot is fired by humanism's rebellious hordes,
Jesus Christ will tower over the ages as
King of kings and Lord of lords.

A.B.B.

CPSIA information can be obtained
at www.ICGtesting.com
Printed in the USA
BVHW032223050421
604304BV00003B/20